Speakeasy: talking with your children about growing up

fpa

putting sexual health on
the agenda

Essex County Council Libraries

Published by

fpa
50 Featherstone Street
London EC1Y 8QU
Tel: 020 7608 5240
Fax: 0845 123 2349

www.fpa.org.uk

The Family Planning Association is a registered charity, number 250187, and a limited liability company registered in England, number 887632.

© **fpa** 2009

Illustrations by Ed Hillyer, Woodrow Phoenix, Corinne Pearlman and Suzy Varty © Comic Company 2009.

Designed by Third Column. Printed by Newnorth.

Crown copyright material is reproduced under the terms of the Click-Use Licence.

ISBN: 978-1-905506-63-7

This book can only give you basic information about sexual health. The information is based on evidence-guided research from the World Health Organization, The Faculty of Sexual and Reproductive Healthcare of the Royal College of Obstetricians and Gynaecologists and The British Association of Sexual Health and HIV available at the time this book was printed. Different people may give you different information and advice on certain points. Remember – contact your doctor, practice nurse or a contraception clinic if you are worried or unsure about anything.

Contents

Acknowledgements

We would like to thank all the people who have contributed their valuable time and knowledge to this book:

- Susie Wood, who wrote the book.
- All the **fpa** staff who commented on early drafts.
- Sue Allen, FFLAG, for her help with Chapter 6.

A special thanks to all the parents who kindly gave their time to be interviewed for this book and to those parents who gave their comments on an early draft, including:

Sandra Beswick
Ruth Burrows
Julie Dawson
Sarah Haddon
Wendi Hart
Diane Heath
Clare Hopkins
Jan Jesson
Jacquie John
Alison Lucas
Suzy Mackie
Roger Miller
Carson Nicoll
Kylie Nixon
Antoinette Sallah
Jez Shea
Lea Tatham
Helen Williams.

Foreword

Maybe your child is very young and has only just begun to ask questions such as "where do babies come from?". Perhaps your daughter has just started her periods, or maybe your children are teenagers and you've realised that you have no idea if they really know about contraception or how to tell someone they're not ready to have sex.

Whatever stage they're at research has shown that children want to be able to talk to their parents about sex and relationships and that the information they get from school is often inadequate. Worryingly, children often get the little they know from friends or even, as they get older, from pornography. So this is where you can come in by reading this incredibly informative book from **fpa**. **fpa** is a respected sexual health charity that has been around for more than 75 years so definitely knows what it's talking about! **fpa** has put together this book after running Speakeasy courses for parents and carers over many years. Parents taking the course have left equipped with the skills they need to talk to their children about growing up. Interviews with their children have shown how much they appreciate the extra support their parents have been able to give them.

If you read this book you can fill gaps in your own knowledge – just because you've managed to have children doesn't mean you know everything there is to know about sex and relationships. If you don't have time to read it all pick out the sections that suit your family at the moment as the book has been designed to be dipped into. It's also full of hints and tips on how to start and continue talking with your children, including how to overcome embarrassment. You'll find lots of stories from other parents who've been through it all and can share with you how they tackled sometimes funny, sometimes difficult situations.

Your children need you to help them grow up safely and with confidence.

I hope you enjoy this book, and find it useful. I certainly did.

Dr Miriam Stoppard

Introduction

The aim of this book is to help you – parents, grandparents, step parents, foster carers, carers – talk with your child about sex and relationships and growing up. This book has been written for adults so we're not suggesting you give it to your child to read. Instead we hope you will read the book on your own, and for the times when you want to look at information with your child, we've included details of useful websites and resources you can look at together. If your child is old enough you might want to suggest they look at these resources on their own.

The idea for this book came from **fpa**'s work with parents and carers on our Speakeasy courses, which have been running in UK communities since 1995. Speakeasy courses involve group work sessions that help parents and carers build the knowledge, confidence and skills they need to talk with their children about sex and relationships – a subject that children need to know about, but parents and carers often find difficult to discuss.

Parents and carers who have completed the Speakeasy course say they feel more confident in:

- their own knowledge of growing up, sex and relationships
- talking with their children about sex and relationships
- identifying situations in every day life when they can bring up the topic of sex and relationships
- answering their children's questions confidently and without embarrassment.

As one parent/carer put it, "The course gave me the confidence to be able to speak with my daughter about periods, pregnancy etc. I don't think I would have been able to do that six months ago, and it's given me the confidence for the future when my children are older."

You can find more information about Speakeasy at the end of this book.

But this book isn't just for parents and carers who have done a Speakeasy course. This book is for **every** parent and carer who wants to be able to talk openly and honestly with their child, and to help them make informed, safe choices when it comes to sex and relationships.

This book gives you information about:

- the physical and emotional changes that occur in boys and girls as they go through puberty
- reproduction – how pregnancy happens
- sex and safer sex – helping to protect against sexually transmitted infections and pregnancy
- relationships
- pregnancy choices, including abortion
- sexuality including lesbian, gay, bisexual and transgender sexuality
- what schools teach about sex and relationships.

It also gives you suggestions on how to answer the questions your child is likely to ask, and how to answer appropriately for their age.

At the end of most chapters you'll find a Useful organisations box which suggests organisations and websites you can contact for further information on the particular subjects raised in that chapter. You'll find all the contact details for those organisations listed in Chapter 13: Useful organisations.

Talking about sex can feel difficult or embarrassing, especially if you received little or no sex and relationships education yourself. But sex is a natural part of life – your child wouldn't be here without it – and it is natural for children to ask questions about it.

This book will help you approach sex and relationships education not as an embarrassing and difficult subject, but as something that can be discussed openly whenever the topic comes up.

> **Throughout this book we talk about parents and carers. You will find that we often use the term parents to refer to anyone who is looking after a child, including mothers, fathers, grandparents, step parents, partners and foster carers.**

Why talk to your children about sex and relationships and growing up?

CHAPTER 1

What this chapter covers

- How sex and relationships education can benefit children.
- Giving your child age-appropriate information.
- Helping to build your child's self-esteem and confidence.
- Helping young people take control of their sexual health.

There are good reasons to talk with your child about sex and relationships, and it doesn't have to be as hard as you think.

Good sex and relationships education can:

- raise the age young people first try out sexual activity[1]
- make young people aware of how to avoid unwanted pregnancy and abortion
- make young people aware of how to avoid sexually transmitted infections.

It can also help young people:

- with their emotional development
- explore their own beliefs about sex and where these fit in with their own cultural and religious beliefs
- stay safe

---

1 Swan C et al, *Teenage Pregnancy and Parenthood: a Review of Reviews, Evidence Briefing* (Health Development Agency, 2003) and Kirby D, *Emerging Answers 2007: Research Findings on Programs to Reduce Teen Pregnancy and Sexually Transmitted Diseases* (National Campaign to Prevent Teen and Unplanned Pregnancy, 2007).

- respect others
- feel more confident talking about sex with their friends and partners when they're older.

Talking with children early about sex and relationships and growing up can feel scary, but if you pitch your advice and answers to your child's level of understanding, you will make it easier for yourself and clearer for your child. For example, a five-year-old doesn't need to know how to use condoms – they are more interested in knowing about their own body and noticing differences between themselves and others.

Sex and relationships education covers a huge area and is not simply about passing on information about growing up and safer sex.

A report into personal, social and health education (PSHE) found that many young people said their parents are not very good at talking about the more sensitive issues, such as sex and relationships.[2] The report recognises that most parents play a significant role in supporting and advising their children, but also that parents have not received sufficient guidance and support to deal successfully with these aspects of PSHE.

"When I was 17 my mum sat me down with an anatomy book and showed me a picture of a womb – she told me about periods and that's where she left it. She didn't tell me about the actual sex bit. I wish there had been a bit more dialogue, especially for when you do have your first sexual encounter. I thought, 'what's going on? ... this wasn't in the picture of the womb!' There was no sex and relationships education at school either. I went to a strict Catholic school and they absolved themselves of all responsibility. Our family ethos now is to be open. There's a lot more pressure on kids these days, including bullying and drugs, and I want my kids to know they can talk to me about anything."

Mother of a son, aged 20 months, and a daughter, aged three

If you don't tell them, someone else will

If children don't learn about sex and relationships from you, they'll certainly pick up messages from their friends, TV or magazines. These messages may be inaccurate, misleading and confusing. By talking with your children you can help them to make sense of this information, put them right, and make sure they haven't got some strange, wrong or risky ideas.

2   Ofsted, *Time for change? Personal, Social and Health Education* (Ofsted, 2007).

> "When I was young you couldn't bring up sex in any way, shape or form with my mum. I think it's really sad. I didn't know anything about periods. I thought you went deaf when you got your periods because that was the rumour on the estate where I grew up. I was dreading starting. I didn't know anything, and I think I was very lucky to have been alright, I really do."

Mother of two sons, aged 28 and 15, and two daughters, aged 12 and seven

Young people want to know about sex and relationships

Young people often report that their sex and relationships education (SRE) happens too late – after they have begun puberty and experienced sexual desire or sex.[3] It makes sense to ensure your children have all the information they need in plenty of time for them to look after themselves and deal with the changes of growing up.

Many children do not receive adequate education about puberty – one in ten girls begin their periods without having any information from their parents or school.[4]
In one UK survey of over 20,000 young people aged under 18, 40 per cent thought the SRE they had received was either poor or very poor, 61 per cent of boys and 70 per cent of girls reported not having any information about personal relationships at school and 73 per cent felt that SRE should be taught before the age of 13.[5]

Young people believe that the SRE they do get focuses too much on biological aspects, such as reproduction, and they would really like the opportunity to discuss feelings, relationships and what leads on to sex.

Remember that just because they are curious about sex doesn't necessarily mean they are having sex, or even interested in having sex yet. Try not to react in a shocked or angry way if your child asks a question about sex; if you do, they may well decide that you do not want to talk about sex with them, and they won't come to you for help in the future.

---

3   Sex Education Forum, *"Please Minister Can We Have Better Sex Education?" – Young People Give Their Views on Sex Education* (Sex Education Forum, 2000) and UK Youth Parliament, *Sex and Relationships Education: Are you Getting it?* (UK Youth Parliament, 2007).

4   Prendergast S, *"This is the Time to Grow Up". Girls' Experiences of Menstruation in Schools* (**fpa**, 1994).

5   UK Youth Parliament, *Sex and Relationships Education: Are You Getting it?* (UK Youth Parliament, 2007).

You can prepare yourself for answering your child's questions by making sure you know the facts yourself. Listen to your child's question, and make sure you know what it is they are asking. This will help you pitch your answer at the right level for what they want to know.

If you weren't given supportive and honest information about sex and relationships when you were growing up you can probably remember how scared and confused you felt. Talk with your children and help them have a more positive experience.

> Yeah, because before it used to be embarrassing but now that I've found out that she knows about it so I can ask her things.
>
> *Son*

> She's been more confident, she can talk about stuff like that now. I've always been confident; I just start talking about stuff like that... She was alright but she didn't really like, talk about it that much until you, like, asked something but now she just says stuff without you having to. It's like vice-versa now.
>
> *Daughter*

Having a parent who is open about sex and relationships issues can help young people have a mature attitude themselves:

> People at school talk about it like it's something dirty and sordid but I just read that [the Speakeasy course material] and it was different and wasn't embarrassing.
>
> *Daughter*

"SRE at school was very basic, we had frogs and flowers; and at home it was not a subject we discussed. I was very naïve, I didn't know anything about boys or getting pregnant except what I heard in the playground – it was all very scary. And I didn't know anything about periods; when I started it was awful. I didn't know what to use so I went to my friend's house. She had already started her periods so she helped me. I didn't tell my mum for a couple of months. Looking back I think it was bloody awful, which is why I don't want my kids going down the same road. Being open about sex is a family thing for us – we want our kids to be able to come and talk to us about anything."

Mother of a daughter, aged three, and two sons, aged four and 19 months

"My sex and relationships education was very limited. My mum died when I was young, and my dad's idea on sex education was 'well, I learned the hard way, you can too'. He didn't really give me any help or advice."

Father of a son, aged 18, and a daughter, aged 12

Give your children the right message

You'll give out messages to your children whether you speak with them about sex and relationships or not. If you don't talk with them about growing up when they're young, or you shy away from the topic when it's brought up:

- they'll pick up the message from you that sex is scary and shouldn't be talked about

- they may find it difficult to ask questions later about anything that worries or confuses them

- they may think that you find it too dirty or embarrassing to talk about.

Give them confidence

The messages young people get from their friends, TV and magazines may lead them into situations they don't know how to cope with. Young people need the information, confidence and skills to handle these pressures.

They need to understand how their bodies and feelings will develop and how those changes might affect them. They need to feel good about themselves and develop the skills to form good friendships and sexual relationships when they are older. If they don't get good information from the right people when they're young they could grow up to have negative experiences of sex and relationships.

Knowing about their bodies and not being surrounded by mystery when it comes to sex and relationships will help your children feel more confident about themselves and their behaviour.

Help your children stay safe

Talking with your child about sex and relationships from an early age also gives you the chance to explain inappropriate adult behaviour towards children. Have a look at Chapter 11 for lots of information on how you can help your children keep safe.

Useful organisations

- **fpa**
- www.likeitis.org.uk
- Parentline Plus
- Sex Education Forum

How do I start and carry on talking about growing up?

CHAPTER 2

What this chapter covers

- How to start talking with your child.
- When to start.
- What to say.
- Finding out what your child already knows.
- How to make talking about sex and relationships easier.
- Supporting your physically impaired child.
- Supporting your learning disabled child.

Lots of people find they get embarrassed when they talk about sex and relationships. It's okay to tell your child you're embarrassed – by acknowledging it you are being honest and they can learn to trust you and know that it's okay to be embarrassed too.

If you react to your embarrassment by avoiding the subject of sex and relationships, or by not answering your child's questions, then they will pick up the message that sex is not something you want to talk about.

You can still help your child learn about sex even if you don't feel very comfortable talking about it.

Some ways of making it easier are:

- **Start early.** You will find it much less embarrassing if you start talking about sex and relationships when your child is very young as young children don't need very detailed information and this is a good way to start. Answer questions simply and naturally, as if you were talking about ice-cream or cars. You don't have to say much. Most children are happiest learning in small steps. For example, if your child asks "How does a baby get in mummy's tummy?" you could say, "daddy puts a seed in there and it begins to grow". We give some more tips about talking to children when they're very young later in this chapter.

- **Use everyday situations to start conversations.** Use TV characters and situations to spark off a chat about sex and relationships – someone is always falling in and out of love in soaps. Or if you see a pregnant woman walking along the street, you could use this to start a chat about where babies come from. This kind of approach will help your child feel that sex is a normal part of family life.

- **Talk when you're doing something else, such as the washing up.** This makes it an everyday topic and not a special subject. Also, if you get embarrassed, you might find it easier to talk if you're busy doing something else.

- **Use humour.** This doesn't mean you need to make jokes all the time, but if you show your child that you can talk and laugh about sex and relationships like any other subject, it will help them to see this as a normal topic. It will have a more positive effect than the kind of humour that is based on embarrassment and ignorance, and that limits sex and relationships to 'naughty' jokes in the school playground.

- **Get some books or leaflets or find a good website**. Your child can look at these on their own but it can be useful if you look at these together. **fpa** has a range of booklets for young people about growing up and sex and relationships (see Chapter 14: Useful resources). There are lots of other good books, leaflets and websites about most aspects of sex and relationships and growing up. Looking at them together can help if you find yourself getting embarrassed because the story can do the talking. You'll both have the same information in front of you – it also means you won't have to think of all the answers for yourself. Before sharing a book, leaflet or website with your child, have a look at it yourself first. That way you can prepare yourself for the questions your child might ask, and you can ensure that it is appropriate.

- **Have a phrase ready for inappropriate moments**. You've probably been in the supermarket queue when your child has suddenly asked how babies are made. If it's not the right moment to deal with it, try saying "that's a good question, let's talk about it when we get home". And make sure you do.

What does your child already know?

Find out how much your child already knows – this can help you give answers they can understand. Don't just give your child a one-off talk about sex and relationships – build on it gradually. Start when they're small and carry on until they have grown up. If you show your child that you are happy to talk about sex and relationships and feelings, they will know they can ask you questions about anything they don't understand.

Finding the right words

Children can often ask questions that are difficult to answer due to their age or your own fear and embarrassment. It is sometimes hard to know how much information to give and you might be worried about giving too much, too soon.

- Make sure you know exactly what they are asking. "Where do I come from?" could mean they want to know what town they live in, not necessarily how babies are made.

- Giving young children short answers may lead them to ask more questions or they may be happy with what you've told them.

- If they ask more questions it's often because they are ready for more information.

- If they ask the same question again, it is often because they have not understood your answer.

- If they change the subject completely or accept the answer it's because they're happy with it.

Many parents feel more comfortable using informal terms for genitals with their young children. As well as using words such as 'willy' or 'minnie' it's good to introduce the terms penis and vagina gradually so that children become more comfortable with these words. If you are not used to saying these words, try saying them out loud by yourself so that it won't feel strange when you teach them to your child.

If your child asks you a question and you don't know the answer, or if you're not sure, say so. But do tell them you will find out and give them the answer later.

Try to be truthful as children get very confused by made-up stories, such as storks dropping babies on the doorstep or babies being found in gooseberry bushes. It's important that children believe what you tell them and have confidence in what you say.

It is also a good idea to try to explain things as clearly as you can, and to avoid half-truths. Children can interpret what you say very literally.

One parent attending a Speakeasy course told of the time her child asked where he had come from. "You came out of mummy's bottom," she replied. Her child thought for a moment before asking, "Was I all dirty then?". He thought he had come out of her anus – illustrating that children can take your answers at face value.

Avoid gender stereotyping

When it comes to sex and relationships education, try not to think in terms of 'what girls need to know' and 'what boys need to know'. You can tell boys and girls exactly the same information – there is no reason for children not to know what happens to boys **and** girls. This knowledge will mean there is no mystery or confusion surrounding growing up, sex and relationships. Your child will know the facts from you, and will be less likely to believe any rumours or half-truths they hear in the playground.

Try not to make assumptions about what your child is going through because of their gender. Remember that boys as well as girls might be concerned about body shape; girls as well as boys might masturbate; boys and girls need to know about periods and how pregnancy occurs. By making it clear that whatever your child is going through is normal, you can help them to feel supported and to avoid feelings of isolation.

> My daughter does like to fiddle with her bits! She's three, and as soon as she takes her knickers off at bath time she's touching herself. My husband can't bear it, but we want to try to make her feel comfortable about her body and not put social conditioning on her, telling her it's bad. The automatic reaction is to say, 'stop doing that!', but instead I say to her that her fingers aren't clean so it's best to wait until she's in the bath. I'm not trying to stop her from finding out what's where or what feels funny and what doesn't.
>
> *Mother of a daughter, three, and a son, 20 months*

Talking with children within the context of religious and/ or cultural views

You may have religious or other views about sex and relationships which you want to introduce to your children. For example, you may believe that people should only have sex when they're married or in other committed relationships.

If you are bringing your child up within a particular faith they still need clear information about sex and relationships, and you can give them this in the context of your faith. Your child needs to know about puberty and the changes that will happen as they grow up. As a responsible parent you can help your children find out all the good things about their sexuality and how to stay safe.

> I was brought up in the Roman Catholic faith and have always believed that life started at the point of conception. I think it's a real tragedy that there are so many abortions although I know that sometimes it's the only realistic choice a woman or girl has. I'm still not quite sure what I think about this – but doing the Speakeasy course gave me the confidence to present information about contraception to my children and when it comes to it – it will be their choice what they decide to do.
>
> *Mother of two daughters, aged 11 and nine*

You also need to let your children know that even if they don't share the same beliefs as you they can always come to you for support.

> "I had some sex education from my mum. In our culture, African culture, we don't really talk about it, but I was lucky. My mum was a teacher and I was really close to her. She talked about it a lot, and I have an older sister who helped. I knew about periods and how to deal with them."
>
> *Mother of three sons, aged 11 years, five years and 21 months*

How do I talk with very young children?

Babies learn their first lessons about feelings from being cuddled and cared for by their mum, dad or carer in addition to watching the world and others around them. So it's important to show affection to your baby with hugs and kisses. Children think that whatever goes on in their family must be the right way of doing things. So don't be afraid to kiss and hug your partner in front of your children, if you want to.

As babies grow, they begin to explore the world around them, often wanting to touch objects or put them in their mouths. When they explore their own bodies they will touch themselves, including their genitals. If you accept that this is normal your baby will learn that **all** of their body is okay. If you tell them off or discourage them, they'll start to feel that their genitals are bad.

Talking with children aged from 3–4

"My young daughter understands that men and boys have willies, and girls and ladies have minnies. This came about after her dad took her out for the afternoon. They both needed the toilet and so he naturally took her to the gents. A couple of days later I noticed her standing over her potty squeezing and pushing her outer lips forward. When I asked her what she was doing, she replied 'weeing like daddy'. This prompted me to explain that men have willies and wee like this, and women have minnies and wee sitting down."

Mother of a daughter, three

By this age children are aware and curious about the differences between the sexes. They may like to peep under each other's clothes, undress their dolls and check out their pets' bottoms. They may enjoy playing 'doctors and nurses' or 'mummies and daddies'. Children start to ask questions about babies. Often they just need the name of something and are happy with short, simple, truthful answers as detailed explanations go over their heads. For example:

Where do babies come from?

A woman and a man have a special cuddle and then the baby grows inside the woman's tummy, safe and warm, until the baby is born.

Can men have babies?

Babies can only grow in a special place inside women's tummies but not in men's tummies.

How does the baby get in?

A man and a woman have a special cuddle and the man's seed reaches a tiny egg in the mummy's tummy.

At this age children may touch their genitals. This is a good time to teach them about the difference between what's acceptable to do in private and public. You can also start teaching them about when touching is wrong and what to do if someone touches them in a way they don't like. See Chapter 11 for more information.

Reading them stories can be a good way of talking about different feelings and relationships.

What would you do if...

You find your four-year-old daughter looking down the pants of the four-year-old boy next door.

This is normal behaviour for curious young children and is one way they learn about themselves and others. It's safe as long as it happens between children approximately the same age and nobody gets hurt physically or emotionally. You can use this as an opportunity to:

- chat about differences between boys and girls
- answer their questions
- gently talk with them about what is acceptable to do in public and private.

"When she was three my daughter started asking about willies all the time, because her brother had just been born. I think she knew I cringed, because she asked all the time – in the post office, in the butcher's, 'Does he have a willy?' I just tried to answer without making a big deal of it. It was a case of, 'Yes, and I'll take a pack of sausages please'. The poor butcher hated it!"

Mother of a daughter, three, and a son, 20 months

Talking with children aged from 5–8

- At these ages children start to learn what their bodies can and can't do and like to find out how things work and how they're made.
- They are curious about their own and other people's bodies, and pregnancy and childbirth.
- They may ask about puberty changes and periods.
- They continue to play games such as 'doctors and nurses', and explore their own and each other's bodies, including the genitals.

This is all normal.

This is a good time to build on what you're already beginning to teach your child about growing up. Some girls start having periods at eight years old so it's best to tell boys and girls about periods by this age. Remember, don't make a big deal of it, for example, when out shopping take your child past the tampons and sanitary towels. It's important to tell boys about periods too.

Children need to know that their bodies will be changing. If you talk with your child you will find out what they already know and what they want to know.

Talking with children aged 9–13

Some children begin to show signs of puberty at this age and become conscious of the differences between their bodies and those of their friends. They may become anxious about what is normal. At this age they're likely to want more information about the changes their body will be going through.

Talking with older children

Young people may pretend they know all about sex – in reality they probably don't.

You can ask them what they know – and fill the gaps. Ask if there's anything else they want to know. Help them by making it easy for them to ask you questions. They may not ask much, but you will have shown that you're understanding, approachable and a good listener.

At this age, children need to know about:

- Puberty changes and body parts.
- Sex and reproduction – they may be hearing about oral and anal sex, and may ask you about these.
- Sexual orientation.
- Contraception and sexually transmitted infections.
- Pregnancy choices, including abortion.
- Periods, wet dreams, masturbation. They may also learn about pornography, and you might need to be prepared to talk about this if the subject comes up.
- Relationships, including the different sorts we have with different people (friends, relatives, people we're in love with), and negotiating relationships.

It is important to explain to young people that being responsible about sex and relationships means considering the needs and feelings of their partner, and talking with their partner.

They need to know that they should:

- not pressure their partner to have sex
- not give in to pressure to have sex themselves, if they're not ready
- talk with their partner about using a condom to help avoid getting a sexually transmitted infection
- use contraception unless they both want a baby.

Teenagers often find it much harder than younger children to talk with their mum, dad or carer about sex and relationships so it helps if you have already talked with children when they were much younger.

However, it's never too late to start talking with your child about sex and relationships, but it may be harder to talk with a teenager if you've never brought the subject up before, as they may already know a lot and become embarrassed. You may have to accept that your teenager doesn't want to talk with you about sex and relationships – it doesn't mean that you're a failure as a parent. But try to make sure they know who they can talk to if they don't want to talk to you, for example, a school nurse, a counsellor at college, a nurse at their general practice, staff at a clinic, another trusted adult or one of the many helplines listed in Chapter 13.

Becoming independent

Part of the process of growing up involves becoming more independent of parents. Young people need privacy and to start making their own decisions. They also need to know you will offer support, advice and friendship when they need it.

Think ahead about how you would react in some situations before they happen so that you can deal with them calmly when they do. Talk them through with family or friends if this helps.

Talking with your son/daughter if you are their mother/father

Some fathers find the thought of talking with their daughters about sex and relationships particularly embarrassing, and likewise some mothers feel the same about talking with their sons. While it can be tempting to respond to your child's questions by saying "Ask your father/mother" you won't be helping your child or yourself to communicate naturally about sex and relationships and they may be reluctant to come to you for support and advice in the future.

Talking with a child of the opposite sex to you doesn't need to be any more difficult than talking with a child of the same sex, particularly if you start talking while your child is still young. All the tips in this book apply. If possible, try and share what you have talked to your children about with their mother/father so you can be consistent in the messages and information you give them.

However, as children get older, you may find that young people prefer to talk to someone who is the same sex as them. Don't be upset by this, many young people start to want more privacy as they go through puberty, particularly around issues such as body changes, wet dreams, masturbation and periods. If your child's mum or dad isn't around to help talk with them about sex and relationships then you could try asking a good friend or relative to talk with your child, if both are comfortable with that, or try asking the school nurse.

> "My daughter recently started her menstrual cycle and her reaction was, 'No, I can't talk to dad about that!'. Her mum asked her why, and she said it was a girl thing. But now my daughter is comfortable letting me know she's on her period."
>
> *Father of a son, aged 18, and a daughter, aged 12*

Talking with your grandchildren

If you are a grandparent, try to be prepared for your grandchild to ask you questions about growing up, sex and relationships. Sometimes children can feel more comfortable talking with their grandparents than with their parents, or sometimes you might just happen to be the person who is around when your grandchild asks a question.

You can use this book to build up your knowledge about sex and relationships, and your confidence in talking about the topic, so that you can feel comfortable talking with your grandchild. Keep the channels of communication open between you and your grandchild by making sure they know they can come to you if they want to know anything.

If you like, you can talk with your grandchild's parents to let them know you are happy to talk about sex and relationships with your grandchild if the subject comes up. You can also ask whether they are using any particular books or words with their child, so that you don't confuse your grandchild by using different words.

Talking with your foster child

As a foster carer looking after a young person in public care, you may sometimes be unsure about what information and advice you can give about issues to do with sex and relationships, including contraception. The Teenage Pregnancy Unit issued guidance about this in 2004.[6] This guidance explains that:

- young people in care have the same right to confidential contraceptive and sexual health information and advice as other teenagers
- young people who are, or are thinking about becoming sexually active, should be encouraged to seek sexual health and contraceptive advice
- any concerns about confidentiality should be addressed
- young people should be directed to local services.

---

6 Teenage Pregnancy Unit, Department for Education and Skills, *Enabling Young People to Access Contraceptive and Sexual Health Information and Advice: Legal and Policy Framework for Social Workers, Residential Social Workers, Foster Carers and Other Social Care Practitioners* (DfES publications, 2004).

During your assessment and induction period as a foster carer, you should have received policies and guidance about these issues. If you are in any doubt then you should contact your social worker who will be able to help you and provide relevant guidance.

If your child has a physical impairment

Young people with physical impairments may have particular sex and relationships concerns, for example they may worry they won't physically be able to have sex or may have issues with self-esteem.

Supporting your physically impaired child through adolescence

Young people with physical impairments need access to the same information about sex and relationships as any young people but they may need additional support around their physical and mental wellbeing. For example, they may have had more clinical tests on their body than other young people and this can affect the way they see themselves as a sexual being as they may be used to a medical approach to their body.

Some young people may need the help of a physiotherapist or clinical practitioner while others may need therapeutic support to help them develop as sexual beings. Don't assume that your son or daughter will not be able to have sex and relationships and don't be scared of involving other professionals who may be able to help – with your son's or daughter's permission of course. They may also be able to get professional help to develop their communication skills so that they can gain the confidence and skills to address personal and relationship issues with a partner.

Your son or daughter may have picked up myths and negative messages about their ability or their right to have a sexual relationship so talk to them about any comments that they may have received and help dispel those myths. As young people with physical impairments are all different, it is important to talk about your child's particular concerns in relation to their own issues.

Getting advice and support for your physically impaired child

There are sources of help available for parents. You could try contacting:

● Other parents who have similar experiences to your own and meet in informal networks and social gatherings.

● Voluntary organisations with a local group which can offer support. You can find details at the local library, or from your child's school or college or try contacting your local children with disabilities team.

● Organisations that specialise in a specific impairment. Contact a Family can advise who to contact.

If your child has a learning disability

Your child will reach puberty and develop into an adult, whatever their learning ability. Girls will start their periods and be able to get pregnant, boys will have erections and ejaculate, and both will have sexual feelings.

As children grow up they are faced with all sorts of new experiences. You can help them to be more independent by trying not to protect them too much. They will learn from these experiences, especially if they are allowed to take some carefully planned risks. You have to work out what you can safely support them to do without them getting into real difficulties.

One of your chief anxieties about your learning disabled child is likely to be that they can be vulnerable to all sorts of exploitation and abuse. But if you teach your child about sex and relationships you can help them to keep themselves safe, so that they know that some parts of their bodies are private, and they will learn what to do and say in certain situations.

Supporting your learning disabled child as they reach adolescence

Adolescence is a particularly challenging time if your child has a learning disability. You may be watching their developing sexuality and maturity with mixed feelings; glad that they are growing up but anxious about what these developments may bring. You may secretly hope that your child will never become interested in sex, with the potential complications it may bring. Or you might become so anxious about the vulnerability of your child that you are reluctant to allow them any kind of independent life.

It's right to want to help your child to avoid being exploited or hurt – that's common to all parents but it is important to remember that ignorance never protects. There are well established ways of teaching young people with learning disabilities the essential information they need about sex and proven methods of helping them to learn the skills they need to manage all their relationships successfully:

- how to greet and behave appropriately with different people
- how to make choices
- how to assert themselves so that they can avoid difficult situations.

And part of that necessary learning is about how to protect themselves in sexual situations.

This may not be relevant for some young people with learning disabilities, but many adults with learning disabilities can enjoy a satisfying sexual partnership which enhances many aspects of their lives. For their protection they will need to understand about avoiding unplanned pregnancies, and avoiding sexually transmitted infections. Because they learn more slowly than others, it's essential that learning about sex and relationships begins early. Schools can introduce the basic knowledge about how bodies work and grow as soon as children enter school; and a good school programme will carry on throughout the years until they leave. But the learning will be faster and longer lasting if it is shared with the adults at home, each reinforcing what the other is doing.

Getting involved with your learning disabled child's school

A good school will take care to involve you in this, consulting you and letting you know what is being taught. You can take an active part in this. It's a good idea to find out from the school the words they are using to describe body parts and the visual and other materials they use. Perhaps ask them to let you know what they are doing in a regular newsletter. Some schools run workshops for parents so that they can talk about their views and their anxieties. Schools can often suggest books and other materials that parents can use at home and some schools have a lending system for this. It's worth making enquiries.

There are other sources of help available to parents. You could try contacting:

- Other parents who have similar experiences to your own and meet in informal networks and social gatherings.

- Voluntary organisations with a local group which can offer support. You can find details at the local library, or from school or college, or try contacting your local children with disabilities team or children and adolescent mental health service.

- Organisations that specialise in a learning disability. Contact a Family can advise who to contact.

fpa has a range of resources to use with people with learning disabilities (see Chapter 14).

Getting advice on contraception for your learning disabled child

If the time comes when your son or daughter needs specific advice about contraception, the first person to talk to about this may be your doctor or practice nurse, or you and your child may prefer to go to a contraception clinic or young people's service. You may wish to accompany your child, or another adult may do so, but for a young adult who has a relationship with a partner, it is probably more appropriate if they visit the clinic together, where trained health professionals should be able to help them to make the best decisions. Clients can ask for a longer appointment time at the clinic.

It's also a good idea to introduce young people to condoms by getting some that they can open and examine. Condoms can help protect against pregnancy and sexually transmitted infections (see Chapters 8 and 9 for more information).

"I had mentioned to a wee boy's mummy, 'they're all into the girls aren't they?' and his mummy looked at me, you know like as if, what's she talking about? And I said, you know, 'is he not talking about all the girls and all and about who he'd like to see?' And she said to me, 'he never says anything like that to her!' And she says, 'honestly, I can't believe you said that to me because it hasn't even crossed my mind!' And when I looked at the dance floor there was her son (aged 16) getting jiggy with this girl! I could even see the mummy then looking and it was like a wee switch in her eyes had went on!"

Mother of a son, 16, with learning disabilities

Useful organisations

- **fpa**
- Action for Kids
- The Ann Craft Trust
- www.bbc.co.uk/barefacts
- British Institute of Learning Disabilities
- Contact a Family
- Learning Disabilities Foundation
- Mencap
- Parentline Plus
- Trust for the Study of Adolescence

Test your knowledge

CHAPTER 3

What this chapter covers

- General knowledge quiz on growing up, sex and relationships.
- Quiz on contraception.
- Quiz on sexually transmitted infections.

In this chapter we've included some quizzes so that you can test your own knowledge about sex and relationships, puberty, contraception and sexually transmitted infections. You'll find the answers at the end of this chaper. Have a go – you may be pleasantly surprised at how much you already know or decide you need to brush up on the facts. Don't worry if you find you know less than you thought you did, hopefully by the time you've finished this book you'll have picked up a lot of the answers or know where to go to find them.

General knowledge quiz

1   **Sexual development in girls can start any time between the ages of eight and 14 – true or false?**

2   **Which of the following changes does *not* happen to boys as they go through puberty?**

- growing taller and more muscular
- hair growing on face, arms, legs, chest, genitals and armpits
- voice deepening
- penis and testicles growing bigger
- eyes changing colour.

3   **Which of the following changes does *not* happen to girls as they go through puberty?**

- growing taller
- hips getting broader

- periods starting
- teeth growing
- breasts developing.

---

4 **When does ovulation occur?**

   a when a sperm fertilises an egg after sex

   b when an egg is released in the ovary 10–16 days before the start of the next period

   c when two people fall in love.

---

5 **Can a woman get pregnant if a man withdraws from her vagina before he ejaculates?**

---

6 **You can get sexually transmitted infections through oral sex – true or false?**

---

7 **If a woman thinks she is pregnant, she can buy a pregnancy test at a pharmacy to make sure. Where can she get a free test done? There is more than one correct answer.**

   a a general practice

   b a contraception clinic

   c a genitourinary medicine (GUM) clinic

   d a sexual health clinic

   e most NHS walk-in centres

   f some pharmacies.

---

8 **Name two types of emergency contraception. How long after unprotected sex can they prevent pregnancy?**

---

9 **Can young people go to a sexual health clinic without their parents' knowledge?**

---

10 **Where can people get free condoms?**

You can find the answers on page 36.

Contraception quiz

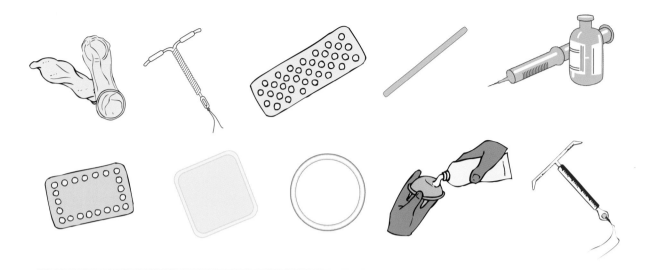

1   **What is the pill containing estrogen and progestogen called?**

   a   the combined pill

   b   the male pill

   c   the mini-pill.

2   **What is the pill containing only progestogen called?**

   a   the combined pill

   b   the female pill

   c   the progestogen-only pill.

3   **At what stage should the male condom be put on?**

   a   while you are making tea

   b   when the penis is erect, before any genital contact and sexual intercourse

   c   after penetration.

4   **The diaphragm and cap are placed where in the body?**

   a   inside the uterus (womb)

   b   inside the vagina to cover the cervix

   c   on your head.

fpa ⦃⦄ Speakeasy: Talking with your chidren about growing up

5   **What is natural family planning?**

   a   having sex without a condom

   b   having sex outdoors

   c   identifying the fertile times of a woman's menstrual cycle.

6   **How does the contraceptive injection work?**
   There is more than one correct answer.

   a   it stops an egg being released (ovulation)

   b   it thickens the cervical mucus and makes the uterus lining thinner

   c   it makes you allergic to your partner.

7   **What do we call the contraceptive method that involves a small progestogen-releasing tube being inserted under the skin of the upper arm?**

   a   the intrauterine system (IUS)

   b   the contraceptive implant

   c   the inner tube.

8   **Which of these methods of contraception can be used as emergency contraception?**

   a   the copper intrauterine device (IUD)

   b   the male condom

   c   the contraceptive implant.

9   **When do you need to take the progestogen-only pill?**

   a   at approximately the same time every day

   b   any time

   c   before sex.

10   **What is involved in male sterilisation?**

   a   the tubes carrying sperm from the testicles to the penis are cut

   b   the testicles are cut off

   c   the man is washed in antiseptic solution every day for a week.

You can find the answers on page 36.

Sexually transmitted infections quiz

1 **Which sexually transmitted infection beginning with the letter 'C' is the most commonly transmitted bacterial sexually transmitted infection? It is sometimes called the silent infection because it can have no symptoms.**

   a chlamydia

   b cholesterol

   c clap.

2 **Which sexually transmitted infection caused by a virus may have visible symptoms of smooth, small or larger cauliflower-shaped lumps around the genital and anal areas?**

   a genital herpes

   b genital warts

   c genital vegetables.

3 **The contraceptive pill provides good protection against sexually transmitted infections as well as being an effective method of contraception – true or false?**

4 **Which sexually transmitted infection beginning with the letter 'G' may be present in the body without any visible symptoms? If there are symptoms, they could include an unusual thin/watery, yellow/green discharge in women, or a white/yellow/green discharge in men?**

   a gonorrhoea

   b gout

   c gastroenteritis.

5 **Name a common viral infection that can cause sores around the genital and anal areas, spread by skin-to-skin contact. These sores can be caused by the same virus that gives you cold sores around the mouth or nose.**

   a the common cold

   b genital herpes

   c genital warts.

6   You can get a sexually transmitted infection the first time you have sex –
    true or false?

7   Can you name a sexually transmitted infection beginning with the letter 'S' that,
    if left untreated, can cause irreversible damage to major organs and death?
    Historical leaders King Henry VIII and Napoleon are thought to have had it.

    a   sore genitals

    b   St Vitus dance

    c   syphilis.

8   Which infection can be passed on through unprotected vaginal, anal or
    oral sex – also through sharing contaminated needles, contaminated blood
    transfusions, childbirth and breastfeeding? There is treatment to control
    symptoms, but there is no cure.

    a   HIV

    b   influenza

    c   MRSA.

9   What method of contraception, when used correctly and consistently, helps
    protect against the spread of HIV and some other sexually transmitted
    infections?

    a   the combined pill

    b   the contraceptive implant

    c   condoms.

10 If you are concerned that you may have a sexually transmitted infection,
    name three places you could go for help and advice.

You can find the answers on page 37.

Answers

General quiz answers

1 True.

2 Eyes changing colour is the wrong answer. Body changes in boys: grow taller and more muscular; shoulders broaden; penis and testicles get bigger; hair grows on legs, arms, face, armpits, genitals and chest; voice deepens.

3 Teeth growing is the wrong answer. Body changes in girls: grow taller; hips broaden; thighs and buttocks fatter; breasts develop; hair grows around genitals, armpits, on the legs and sometimes other parts of the body; periods start.

4 **a** Ovulation is the release of an egg in the ovary. It usually occurs 10–16 days before the first day of the next period.

5 Yes, because sperm can be released before a man ejaculates.

6 True.

7 All the answers are correct. She can buy a test from a pharmacy or can get a test done at a general practice, a contraception clinic, a sexual health clinic, a genitourinary medicine (GUM) clinic, most NHS walk-in centres (England only), some pharmacies.

8 Emergency hormonal contraception (emergency pill) can be taken up to three days (72 hours) after unprotected sex; copper IUD can be inserted up to five days after unprotected sex or ovulation.

9 Yes.

10 You can buy condoms at pharmacies, some supermarkets and vending machines; you can get free condoms from contraception clinics, sexual health clinics and some general practices.

Contraception quiz answers

1 **a** the combined pill

2 **c** the progestogen-only pill

3 **b** when the penis is erect, before genital contact or sexual intercourse

4 **b** inside the vagina to cover the cervix

5   **c**   identifying the fertile times of a woman's menstrual cycle

6   **a**   stops an egg being released (ovulation), **and**
      b   it thickens the cervical mucus and makes the uterus lining thinner.

7   **b**   the contraceptive implant

8   **a**   the copper IUD

9   **a**   at approximately the same time every day

10   **a**   the tubes that carry sperm from the testicles to the penis are cut.

Sexually transmitted infections quiz answers

1   **a**   Chlamydia

2   **b**   Genital warts

3   False

4   **a**   Gonorrhoea

5   **b**   Genital herpes

6   True

7   **c**   Syphilis

8   **a**   HIV

9   **c**   Condoms

10   Genitourinary medicine (GUM) clinic, sexual health clinic, general practice, contraception clinic, private clinic/doctor, hospital.

Useful organisations
- **fpa**

Growing up and puberty

CHAPTER 4

What this chapter covers

- The physical changes that happen to boys and girls during puberty.
- Emotional changes.
- Keeping healthy.

How you feel

Seeing your child growing up can trigger a range of emotions. You might feel proud, or sad, or worried, or a mixture of all these emotions, and more – and this is natural. Try to remember that you can help your son or daughter through puberty by making sure they know what to expect. There are a number of books and organisations that can provide help and support, including **fpa** and Parentline Plus (see Chapters 13 and 14).

How your child feels

Puberty affects young people emotionally as well as physically. Hormonal changes can lead to mood swings, including irritability, tearfulness, and confusion. They may become argumentative or bad tempered, and may challenge authority; they may feel intense emotions of love, happiness, low self-esteem, frustration and apathy.

Extreme feelings of creativity, love, rage and despair are typical of the teenage years because the body is producing high levels of the hormones responsible for these feelings. Some people barely notice the ups and downs; others may swing between exhilaration and despair.

Helping your child build self-esteem

Self-esteem is an important factor in how we live our lives; it can inform the decisions we make and the way we treat ourselves and other people. Helping to build your child's self-esteem can feel like a difficult thing to do, but it doesn't have to be. Self-esteem is all about realising your own unique place in the world, and that the things you think and do have value.

But where do you start? Here are a few suggestions.

Looks

You can help your child understand that everyone is different, and that people's bodies develop in their own unique way. One way is not better than another. You can also teach your child that the idealised way that men and women look on television and in magazines is not realistic. Young men and women can worry about their weight, and can feel negative about themselves. Let them know that how they feel about themselves is more important than how much they weigh or what they look like.

If only …

Sometimes it is easy for teenagers (and adults!) to fall into the trap of thinking 'if only…'. For example, 'my life would be perfect if only I were taller/thinner/had muscles/had perfect skin'.

If your child says something like this, talk with them about it. Ask them gently how they think it would make their life better if they were taller/thinner. Reassure them that what they look like is not the most important thing. What is important is what they are like as a person – the things they think and do and say, and how they treat people. These are why people become friends with them, not for their looks.

Some simple exercises

You can help your child think about their own achievements and good qualities by carrying out the following simple exercises together. **fpa** has used these exercises with groups of 9–13-year-old children, but you can use them with older or younger children, keeping the discussion appropriate to your child's age.

There are no right or wrong answers in these exercises; they are simply a useful tool for opening up discussion about values and the things people do.

The gingerbread man

You will need a piece of paper and a pen. The aim is to give your child the opportunity to think about themselves and their life, and to talk about this with you. If you ask a child outright what they have achieved, or what their good qualities are, they might say 'nothing'. This exercise encourages them to think about their life and achievements and view them from a different perspective.

You can encourage your child by answering the questions yourself, and talking about your life. This makes the exercise two-way, rather than focused purely on your child. It becomes a sharing exercise, and you can learn things about each other.

Draw a gingerbread man on the piece of paper – it doesn't have to be perfect, just good enough to see the arms, legs, body and head.

The feet: where your child has been

Point to the gingerbread man's feet and ask your child, "Where have you been?"

The answers might include school, a friend's house, grandparent's house, on holiday, to an after-school club – anything your child wants to talk about.

Ask your child some questions to open up the discussion, such as:

- What was it like there?
- Who else was there?
- How did it make you feel?
- What did you like about it?
- What didn't you like about it?
- How did you deal with the things you didn't like?
- Did you learn anything interesting there?

The hands: what your child has done

Point to the gingerbread man's hands and ask your child, "What have you done?".

The answers can involve anything including learning to swim, making new friends, helping someone, being in a play at school, doing well in a test, feeding a pet.

Ask your child questions about the things they mention, such as:

- What was it like?
- How did you feel?
- What was the best bit?
- Was there anything you didn't like?
- Did you feel afraid? If so, how did you deal with this?

Talking with you about these things can help your child realise that they have achieved some positive things and deserve to feel proud of them.

The heart: what is important to your child

Draw a heart in the gingerbread man's chest and ask your child, "What do you love?".

The answers can be about anything such as family, friends, music, pets, school, sports, reading, dancing, making things.

Ask your child questions to encourage them to explore these things, such as:

- Why do you like it?
- How does it make you feel?
- What are your favourite things about it?
- Is there anything you don't like about it? If so, how do you deal with this?

Talking like this with your child can help them work out that taking part in things they enjoy is important, and that their passion for the things they love is part of what makes them unique. It can encourage them to see that it is okay to like the things they like, and to do the things they enjoy.

The head: what your child thinks

Point to the gingerbread man's head and ask your child, "What do you think about?".

You can choose topics, such as school or friendship, to start the conversation if you need to.

This can be an effective way to encourage your child to talk and think about their beliefs and values. Be respectful of what they think. Challenge them gently if you want to, but your child needs to know you respect their opinion. If you disagree or tell them they are wrong, they might not want to open up and talk with you in the future.

This discussion can allow your child to explore their ways of thinking and where they fit in with the world, and work out what is important to them.

Photo collage

Another exercise you can carry out with your child involves looking at photographs of him or her.

Gather some photographs of your child taken over the last year or two. Choose a time when you know you won't be disturbed, and sit down with your child to look at the photographs together.

Ask questions to encourage your child to talk about how they have changed, for example:

- What is different about you in these photographs?
- Why do you look different?
- What do you think you might look like in a year's time?
- What can you remember about the day this photograph was taken?
- Who else was there?
- Who took the photo?
- What happened afterwards?
- What was good about that day?
- Was there anything you didn't like about it?
- Would you enjoy doing that kind of thing now?

If you like, you can also discuss photographs of yourself taken over the last year or two so that this becomes a sharing exercise.

When you have looked at all the photographs of your child, make a collage of them together – arrange the photographs on a sheet of paper and stick them down with glue. Frame the collage and hang it in your home in a place where visitors will see it, such as the entrance hall; this can help your child feel that the collage and their history are things to be proud of.

Even taking the time to sit with your child and talk about their thoughts and feelings can make them feel special and loved.

Puberty in young women

Physical changes

- breasts start to grow
- hair grows around the genitals, under the arms, on the legs, and sometimes on other parts of the body
- hips get broader
- thighs and buttocks get fatter
- skin may become spotty
- periods start.

Breasts

Breasts and nipples tingle or itch while they're developing. Your daughter might worry this is not normal, so let her know it is healthy and it will stop once they've grown. Growth can be uneven, so one breast may be bigger than the other. This will even out, but many women have slightly differently sized breasts all their lives.

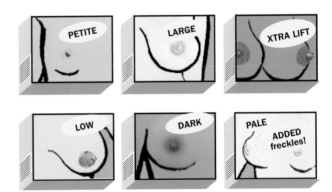

Breasts come in different sizes and shapes. Reassure your daughter (and sons) that all sizes are normal, and no size or shape is better than any other. There is nothing a girl can do to make her breasts develop more quickly, or be smaller or bigger. It is a good idea for girls to get measured at a bra-fitting service so that they will be wearing the correct sized bra – most department stores that have lingerie departments offer this service.

Usually the nipples point outwards, but some young women have nipples that are inverted (point inwards). This is normal, and won't prevent breastfeeding in the future.

Periods

A period is bleeding from the vagina that lasts for a few days – usually around four or five days (although bleeding for a longer or shorter time is normal).

Girls can start their periods anywhere between the ages of eight and 18 years old. Most girls start between the ages of 11 and 15. Periods will start when a girl's body is ready; you can't make them start or stop them from starting. Starting her periods is a sign that changes are happening inside her body, preparing her body for having a baby one day.

Even before birth, a girl has over a million tiny eggs in her ovaries. When she reaches puberty one egg is usually released every month from the ovaries. The release of an egg is called ovulation. The egg is tiny, and moves along the fallopian tubes to the uterus. The uterus is where a baby would grow if the egg were fertilised by sperm from a man.

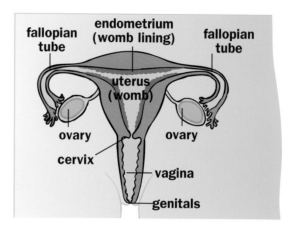

The uterus gets ready for a possible pregnancy each month and its lining becomes thick and soft. If an egg is not fertilised, the endometrium (uterus lining) passes out of the body as blood through the vagina. This is a period.

Helping your daughter manage her periods

A girl needs to know about periods before she starts them, so that she will know that what is happening is normal. Suddenly to discover that she is bleeding can be very frightening if she doesn't know what is happening. Make sure she knows how to deal with her period when it starts; have some sanitary products in the house and let her know where they are and how to use them.

Explain to your daughter that she can use sanitary towels or tampons to collect the blood and allow her to decide which method she finds easiest and most comfortable to use. Some women may choose to use a menstrual cup or sponge. Make sure she knows that she should change the towel or tampon several times a day. She should change a tampon every four hours or sooner and wash her hands before and after doing this. It is important that she remembers to take out her last tampon at the end of her period.

Make sure your daughter knows that sometimes there can be problems with using tampons, leading to a serious illness called toxic shock syndrome. If a girl or woman has two or more of the following while using tampons, she should stop using them and see a doctor straightaway – being sick, a rash, sore throat, sudden fever or diarrhoea.

Depending on your daughter's age, talk about whether she would prefer you to give her the money to buy tampons and sanitary towels herself, or for you to buy them for her.

Explain to your daughter that she may well leave some blood on the sheets or on her pants when she has her period and that it is nothing to be embarrassed about.

If she is worried about everyone knowing she has her period, reassure her that they won't be able to tell. She could always wear dark clothing on the day she thinks her period is due, if it reassures her.

Many fathers feel confident talking to their daughter about periods but if you don't and you are bringing up your daughter on your own you may find it particularly helpful to enlist support from a female relative or friend. She can help explain all the practicalities of managing periods, maybe taking your daughter shopping and helping her choose the appropriate tampons and/or sanitary towels when she first has her period.

The menstrual cycle

The menstrual cycle is the time between one period and the next. Day one of the cycle is the first day of a period, and the last day of the cycle is the last day before the next period begins.

A woman can get pregnant when she ovulates. Ovulation occurs 10–16 days before the start of her period.

Periods usually come around once every month, but a young woman's body needs practice to get this right. For the first year or more the time between her periods may be different. This can make it difficult to know when she will have a period, so it can be a good idea for her to carry sanitary towels or tampons with her all the time or use a pant liner if she thinks she is about to start her period. Suggest she asks a friend, school nurse or teacher if she does get taken by surprise or in an emergency uses paper towels or toilet paper. After a while her periods should become more regular. It can be helpful if she records her periods in a diary so that she can work out when her next period is due.

What would you do if...

Your 14-year-old daughter asks you what she should do as she is very worried that her periods do not come regularly and she bleeds at different times each month. You know that she started her periods six months ago because she told you at the time.

You could tell her that it is normal for some young women to have irregular periods for up to two years after they first start, and you can reassure her that she has done the right thing by talking with you.

The average length of the menstrual cycle is 28 days, although many women have longer or shorter cycles (21 to 40 days) and this is normal. A woman's menstrual cycle won't necessarily be the same as her friends' – her cycle may be longer or shorter, more irregular or more regular, and her periods may be longer, shorter, heavier or lighter. All of this is normal.

"If I'm using the loo and changing a tampon or something, and my four-year-old son comes in and asks what I'm doing, I just say, 'that's for ladies when they're grown up'. He seems very happy with that answer. I want to be open with him, I don't want him to feel anything is hidden."

Mother of two sons, aged four and 19 months, and a daughter, aged three

Period pains

Some women have cramps very low in their stomach when they have a period. Sometimes a painkiller, such as ibuprofen or paracetamol, can help; so can holding a hot water bottle against the stomach. Some women find that exercising helps.

If pains are really bad, a doctor should be able to help.

HPV vaccine

All girls aged 12–13 years are offered an injection which provides protection against HPV, the virus which can cause cancer of the cervix. If you want more information visit www.fpa.org.uk or speak to your daughter's school nurse. The vaccination does not protect against sexually transmitted infections or pregnancy so a condom should be used during sex.

Puberty in young men

Physical changes

- shoulders get broader
- hair grows around the genitals, under the arms, on the legs, chest, back and on the face
- the voice deepens (breaks)
- the penis and testicles get bigger
- ejaculation happens for the first time
- skin may become spotty
- some boys may get sensitive nipples and breasts for a short time.

The penis, erections and testicles

The penis has two main parts: a head (or glans) and a shaft. The head of the penis is much more sensitive than the shaft. Normally a man's penis is soft and hangs down, but if he gets sexually excited (and often when he's not aware of it) he gets an erection:

- the penis goes stiff
- it grows larger and wider
- it sticks outwards and upwards from the body.

Erections (hard-ons, boners, stiffies) can come and go without warning, appearing and disappearing at a moment's notice – sometimes in embarrassing circumstances or at inappropriate moments. The penis fills with blood when a man is sexually excited; there are no bones or muscles in the penis. The shape of an erect penis varies. It usually curves upwards slightly, and may point to one side. Erections occur in males of all ages, including babies and old men.

A penis is used for two jobs: urinating (peeing) and sex. When the penis is erect, a man can't urinate easily because a muscle closes the bladder off.

"My 11-year-old son and I were in the car when he said, 'Dad, I must like fat women'. I asked why, and he said that every time he saw a fat woman he got a boner. I said he'd have to refresh my memory about what a boner is! He said it was an erection. I explained that it didn't mean he only liked fat women, it was just that with a male, an erection can happen several times a day – you could be watching an advert on telly and it'll happen. It's just one of those things. I told him it would ease off, and that it's the same for every boy. I felt fine answering that, and I told him he can come and talk to me about anything. If I don't know the answer, I'll find out."

Father of a son, now aged 18, and a daughter, aged 12

The testicles (balls, bollocks, nuts, nads) hang just behind the penis in a sack of skin called the scrotum. The testicles produce tiny, tadpole-shaped sperm that can fertilise an egg if they get into a girl's or woman's body, and she will get pregnant.

The scrotum is usually darker in colour than the rest of the skin, and is hairy. When it's cold, the scrotum becomes wrinkled; when it's warm, the testicles hang loose and the surface of the scrotum is smooth.

See Chapter 7 for more information on the penis.

Size really doesn't matter

Many young men worry that their penis is smaller than anyone else's. This is unlikely. Adult penises do vary, but not by as much as people think. As a rough rule, the larger a penis is when soft, the less it grows when hard. If it is small when soft, it will probably grow more when hard. Penises when erect are very similar in size for all men. Nothing will make a penis any larger or smaller.

The foreskin

The foreskin is a sleeve of skin that surrounds the head of the penis. When a man gets an erection, the foreskin stretches. The head of the penis is then completely exposed.

Men need to wash under the foreskin, otherwise a creamy, yellow-white substance builds up. This is normal, but if it isn't washed every day it can smell. Young men should be able to pull their foreskin back to expose the head of the penis.

If a young man has a tight foreskin, it can make erections painful. If this is the case, he can **gently** pull the foreskin away from himself while soaking in a warm bath; then he can pull it back and hold in a stretched position briefly. This may gradually stretch the foreskin. If there seems to be a problem, talk with a doctor.

Complete removal of the foreskin is called circumcision. Some men are circumcised, usually for religious reasons. For example, most Jewish and Muslim boys are circumcised in childhood. It makes no difference to a man's ability to urinate or ejaculate.

Looking after the testicles

Spots, moles and bumps are common on the scrotum and penis and don't usually mean anything, but make sure your son knows how to check his testicles. Testicular cancer (cancer of the balls) is the most common cancer in men aged 15–44.[7] Almost

---

7   http://info.cancerresearch.org, accessed August 2008.

100 per cent of all cancers of the testicles can be cured if detected early enough. Every month, your son should:

- feel each testicle in turn, rolling it between his thumb and forefinger
- 'weigh' each testicle in his cupped hand; one should not be heavier than the other
- look out for a dull ache in his testicles; small, hard, painless lumps; one testicle growing heavier or larger than the other; blood coming from the penis.

If he notices any of these things, let him know that a doctor will need to check them out. Reassure him that the doctor will have seen lots of young men like him; let your son know that you can go with him to the doctor if he wants you to.

Sleep

When they are going through puberty, young people need extra sleep. During sleep the body releases growth hormone, which your child needs a lot of during puberty. So while it may seem that your child is being lazy, it might really be that he or she is desperately in need of sleep.

Masturbation

Masturbation is when someone touches, rubs or strokes their own body parts for pleasure. Both girls and boys can do it, and most do at some point. Many people have fantasies while masturbating – this is normal.

Most young men masturbate to get an erection and to have an orgasm (come). Masturbation may start at any age, but it can't lead to ejaculation until boys reach puberty. To masturbate several times a day is not unusual, nor is less often.

Most young men will wake some time or another to find they have ejaculated in the bed – this is a wet dream. It may be embarrassing to mess the sheets but it's completely normal. If they are anxious about this they can wear pants to bed.

Most women masturbate by rubbing/stroking around or on their clitoris and maybe moving their fingers in and out of the vagina. The clitoris is a small fleshy bump at the front of the inner lips which surround the vagina – its purpose is to give sexual pleasure.

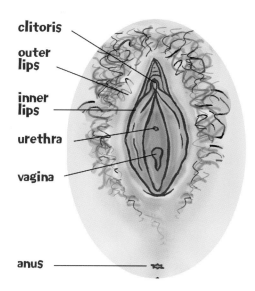

Young men and women who masturbate can learn what they like and can pass this information on to a partner.

It may feel difficult to talk with your son or daughter about masturbation, but they should know that it is normal and won't hurt them. Some children can feel guilty about it, so let them know they do not need to. They also need to know that it's every young person's choice whether to masturbate or not.

Orgasm

In both men and women, an orgasm is a series of muscular spasms followed by relaxation. Orgasm feels very pleasurable.

During a man's orgasm he has rapid, rhythmical contractions which last for several seconds. Each lasts about a second. The first three or so are usually the most intense, and orgasm usually involves ejaculation. Sometimes sperm may be pumped quite a distance, at other times it just dribbles out. See Chapter 7 for more information on male ejaculation.

During a woman's orgasm she may experience a pleasurable throbbing in her pelvis which is brought about by quick rhythmical contractions of muscles in the pelvis, vagina and around the clitoris. Some women find these waves spread through their entire body, while some experience just a small vibration. Others ejaculate a small amount of fluid from their urethra.

Personal hygiene

Young men and women start to sweat more during puberty, and need to wash regularly to stay healthy and avoid smelling. A daily shower or bath is fine, plus another wash after exercise or sport.

In girls, perfumed soaps, bubble baths and shower gels can disturb the normal, healthy environment in the vagina if used on the genitals, and this can lead to irritation or infections, such as thrush. Thrush can cause itching, pain or burning, and a white discharge. It is easily treated with creams, vaginal pessaries (tablets inserted in the vagina) or medicine taken by mouth. If your daughter has any of these symptoms, a doctor will be able to help. Plain, unperfumed soaps are healthiest to use in the genital area.

Be sensitive when talking with your child about personal hygiene and try not to do it in front of their siblings or friends, but don't make an issue out of talking with them on their own. For example, if you notice your child has begun to have body odour, you could talk about it when you are alone in the car or in the kitchen, or watching TV. Try saying something like, "I know that I need to wash every day so that I don't smell. I've had to do it since I was your age, so you might be getting to the age where you need to be washing every day too." Reassure your child there is nothing wrong with sweating, and that it is easily overcome with washing and using deodorant. Talking about the issue in relation to yourself can help prevent your child feeling isolated or embarrassed.

Exercise and diet

For a healthy lifestyle, everyone should aim to eat a healthy diet and get regular exercise – and this is true of teenagers too.

A healthy diet includes:

- carbohydrates, such as bread, pasta, rice or potatoes
- protein (in meat, fish, lentils, beans, tofu or eggs)
- fruit or vegetables (fresh, frozen, tinned, dried, or as juice)
- dairy products (milk, cheese, yoghurt).

Your child should avoid eating too many foods that are high in fat, sugar or salt (for example, fast food, crisps, sweets, chips and fizzy drinks) as these can lead to health issues. If someone eats too much fat and doesn't exercise, they will become overweight, which is associated with problems such as diabetes.

Eating healthy snacks regularly can help to avoid energy slumps and mood swings.

Exercise keeps you fit, tones muscles, can help boost mood, and some activities may help with co-ordination skills. Team sports can be a fun way to keep active, make friends and learn to work with others; there should be teams at your child's school or in the local community.

There are plenty of other activities young people can take part in – walking, running, cycling, tennis, swimming; find out what is on offer at your local leisure centre, or ask your child's school what activities are available.

Spots/acne

Puberty can cause sebaceous glands in the skin to be over-active and to produce too much oil. This can lead to blocked pores, causing spots or acne, especially on the face. The best thing your child can do is to keep their skin clean, and keep healthy generally – eat healthily and get regular exercise. If acne becomes a problem, talk with a doctor. There are drugs on prescription that can help clear up acne, and sometimes the contraceptive pill can help clear up girls' skin too.

Smoking

It is illegal to sell cigarettes or tobacco to people under the age of 18, but there is still a large number of young people who smoke. Research shows that over 80 per cent of adult smokers say they started smoking regularly before the age of 19.[8]

You can teach your child about the dangers of smoking from an early age, so that they understand how it can affect their health. Children who smoke are 2–6 times more likely to get coughs and increased phlegm, wheezing and shortness of breath than those who do not smoke.[9]

Smoking is known to cause lung cancer, and to increase the risk of many other illnesses, including mouth cancer, bladder cancer, emphysema, bronchitis and heart disease.

---

8 Goddard E, *General Household Survey 2006: Smoking and Drinking Among Adults 2006* (Office for National Statistics, 2008).

9 Royal College of Physicians, *Smoking and the Young* (Royal College of Physicians, 1992).

Questions children ask

Age 3–4

Your child asks: Why does my brother squirt spray under his arms after he's had a shower?

You could answer: He does that because he is older than you and his body is changing and getting ready to become a man. He gets sweatier than you do so he uses the spray to help him smell nice and fresh all the time.

Age 5–8

Your child asks: Dad, why is my willy sticking out?

You could answer: Blood goes around your body all the time but sometimes more blood goes into your penis than usual and makes it stick out like that. It's something that happens to all boys and men, even when they are babies.

Age 9–13

Your child asks: My friend was talking about wanking. What does wanking mean?

You could answer: Wanking means rubbing or touching the sexual parts of your body in a way that feels good. Doing this is also called masturbation and it is something that both boys and girls can do if they want.

Useful organisations

- **fpa**
- beat
- Drinkaware
- Eatwell
- Go Smoke Free
- Parentline Plus
- Trust for the Study of Adolescence

CHAPTER 5

Love and relationships

What this chapter covers

- Positive and negative relationships.
- Love, crushes and rejection.
- Different kinds of relationships.
- What makes a good friend.
- Marriage, co-habiting and civil partnerships.
- Splitting up, separation and divorce.

How you feel about your child having boyfriends/girlfriends

When your child gets to the stage of wanting to have a boyfriend or girlfriend, it can be a big step for everybody, but it doesn't have to be difficult. Talk with your child about your beliefs and values when it comes to relationships, and ask what they think. Try not to impose your own beliefs on your child but let them develop their own values. If you build your child's self-esteem and help them learn what makes a good, healthy relationship then you are helping to build the confidence and skills they need to negotiate a relationship.

Having boyfriends or girlfriends can often be a source of tension and arguments in families; young people want to test the limits of their independence, and you may be worried about letting them go. If this is the case, ask yourself what it is you are worried about. Is it that your child may be taken advantage of? That they will get into trouble? That there might be a pregnancy? Whatever the source of your worry, try to find a way to deal with it.

For example, if you are worried somebody will take advantage of your child, you could help your child develop their own assertiveness and confidence. If you are worried about pregnancy, make sure your son or daughter knows how to avoid one, either by not having sex or – if they do have sex – knowing how to get and use contraception.

Try to keep a dialogue open between you and your child so that they can come to you with any worries, and you can be open with them about any concerns.

Think back to when you were a teenager. Chances are you felt you knew how to look after yourself; your child probably feels the same way now, and may well feel hurt or upset if they get the impression you don't think they are capable of looking after themselves. Reassure them that you do trust them but you just want to make sure they know all the facts – for your own piece of mind.

Positive and negative relationships

Young people need to know the difference between a positive and a negative relationship.

Positive relationships

In a positive, caring relationship two people feel good about themselves and each other. Good relationships include things like:

- being good friends
- being able to disagree with each other
- freedom to do your own thing
- time and space to see your friends
- having your own interests
- knowing your opinions are respected
- having fun together
- trusting each other
- being able to go at your own pace – including sexually
- making decisions together
- being able to talk about it when you have an argument
- feeling safe
- respecting the decision if either of you want to end the relationship.

Everyone deserves respect. When it comes to relationships, there is no excuse for violence, abuse or taking advantage of someone.

Negative relationships

In a negative relationship, one person dominates and controls the other. This can include things such as your child's boyfriend/girlfriend:

- getting angry when they talk with someone else
- calling them names, putting them down, making them feel bad
- being verbally aggressive or physically threatening
- using force, threats, emotional blackmail or bargains to make them do things they don't want to do
- posting unpleasant or intimately revealing things about them on the internet
- threatening to harm any of their family, friends, pets or property.

Young people need to know that it is unacceptable if someone treats them in any of these negative ways. If your son or daughter is in an abusive relationship, try to talk with them about it. Let them know you love them and want to help. Make sure they know where they can go for help and support.

Your child might feel love for the person who is abusing them, and it might be very difficult for them to leave the relationship, especially if the abuser has reduced their self-esteem. Help them to find counselling if they need it, or encourage them to contact one of the support organisations below.

- In an emergency, call 999
- Childline
- Get connected
- London Lesbian and Gay Switchboard
- Sexwise
- Supportline
- www.there4me.com.

Love, rejection, broken relationships

Try to remember that young people are capable of falling in love; you might feel they are too young to know what love is, but to young people it is very real and can involve the most intense feelings they have ever experienced. If you tell them that they are too young to be in love, or that their feelings are just a phase, this will not make them feel like confiding in you the next time they need help or advice.

Try to respect their feelings, and the strength of the emotions they are going through. Be aware that young people's relationships can be fairly stormy and involve breaking up and getting back together again several times. This is partly because young people are learning how to negotiate relationships as part of the growing up process – they may not have developed the necessary communication skills to deal with sometimes minor issues in their relationship and see ending the relationship as the only option.

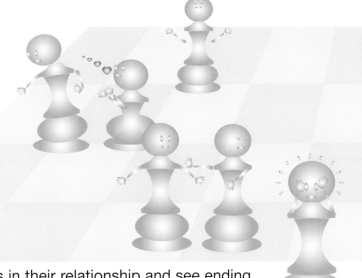

However, if your child goes through a painful relationship break-up, the one certainty is that these feelings will pass, and your child will feel better in time. But how can you help them here and now? Reassure them that you love them and you are there for them. Let them know that sometimes relationships just don't work out; it does not mean there is anything wrong with them as a person, it just means that their boyfriend/girlfriend wasn't the right person for them. It takes two people to make a relationship work, and if one person doesn't want that then the relationship needs to end.

Remind your child that they can fall back on the people who really do love them – their family, friends, even pets. Rejection is part of life, and if they learn from it, it can help their next relationship be smarter and stronger.

Crushes

Talk with your son or daughter about the difference between love and a crush.

A crush can be emotionally all-encompassing, exhausting and unrealistic. The object of a young person's passion may not know their admirer exists or how they feel. If he/she is a celebrity or teacher that's the way it's likely to stay. If it's their sister's best friend, however, there may be a chance of it becoming real.

If young people want to, they can talk with the person they have a crush on, get to know them and find out if they have things in common. A crush becomes love when it becomes real – when they tell the other person how they feel and find out that they feel the same.

If your son or daughter is looking for a relationship and can't find it, encourage them to develop other relationships. People who make and maintain close friendships learn valuable skills to apply next time around to a different kind of love.

Different kinds of relationships

Your child already has lots of relationships in their life – with parents, brothers and sisters, friends, neighbours, teachers and so on. From a young age you can talk with them about different kinds of relationships, and help them to identify healthy qualities in relationships.

For example, what do they look for in a friend or a friendship? You can help them to understand that someone who is mean or makes them feel sad or upset is not someone who makes a good friend. A good friend is supportive, understanding, someone you can be yourself with, and someone who helps you feel good about yourself and life. You could ask your child about the top five qualities they look for in a friend/friendship and help them work out what are the most important qualities from that list.

When it comes to relationships with a boyfriend or girlfriend, the same positive qualities are important. You could try doing the following fun exercise with your son or daughter to help them think about the kind of person they want to get close to. Look at some samples of lonely hearts ads from the soul mates section of magazines or newspapers and talk about the sorts of things people look for in a partner. See if they can come up with five to ten words they would use to describe themselves if they were going to put their own soul mate advert in the paper – you may need to encourage them not to just concentrate on the way they look. Get them to think about what they would look for in a partner and to write a soul mate advert for their perfect partner.

When talking with your child about loving relationships and sex, remember that not everybody has the same sexual orientation. Sexual orientation can take many forms – straight, gay, lesbian, bisexual. A lot of people, including adults, are unsure what their sexual orientation is but remind your child that all people are entitled to live their life being true to their sexual orientation. Your child may know people who are gay, lesbian or bisexual, or they might be discovering that they are not heterosexual themselves.

For more information and sources of support about sexual orientation, see Chapter 6.

What would you do if...

Your child asks: Why doesn't anyone fancy me?

You could answer: How do you know no one fancies you? Most people keep quiet about who they fancy in case that person doesn't fancy them back. You have a great personality and you're lovely to look at and any one would be lucky to go out with you. But you don't need a boyfriend/girlfriend to have a good time, what about all the fun you have with music/sport/going out with your mates?

(It may be appropriate to share your own teenage experiences here).

Marriage, cohabiting, civil partnerships

"My daughter is three and a half and she tells me and her dad that she loves us. She also now says she loves her little brother and wants to live with him and marry him. She knows marrying someone is a symbol of love but she doesn't get that brothers and sisters don't get married. I said to her, 'Well, you live together at the moment so there's no point in getting married yet', and she seems happy with that. I think it's too early to get into explaining incest to her – I have enough trouble explaining why clouds rain!"

Mother of daughter, three, and son, 20 months

From a young age your child will see people in partnerships, and may well ask questions about love, marriage and living together. They may act out marriage in their play. You can explain that when two people have a special kind of love, sometimes they decide to live together, get married or have a civil partnership.

Marriage is a legal union between a man and a woman. A civil partnership is a legal union between two people of the same sex. To get married or to have a civil partnership in the UK, you must be at least 16 years old, but you might need written consent if you are under 18.

Cohabiting is when people decide they want to live together but they aren't married or in a civil partnership. You can explain to your child that people don't have to be married or in a civil partnership to live together or to have children.

For more information about talking with your child about sexuality, see Chapter 6.

Splitting up, separation and divorce

The following information is taken from the Parentline Plus booklet *Splitting up*. You can view their full series of publications at www.parentlineplus.org.uk/publications.

Thousands of children experience the break up of their families every year and divorce and separation can be very painful for the whole family. Whatever your feelings, it is important to put your children's needs first and avoid them being caught up in conflicts and arguments. Family change can be very hard and upsetting for children – but most find that in time, things do get better and they can eventually feel okay about what's happened.

Tips to help you talk with your children about splitting up

- Do reassure your children that it is not their fault and that they are loved by both their parents.

- Do ask for help early on – family, friends and professionals can help you and your children to adapt to changes in your family.

- Do sort out details of contact, residence and finance calmly so that you all know what is happening – it will make it less painful for your children. Local mediation services can help.

- Do be honest with your children about what is happening and what is going to happen.

- Trying to hide conflict or the fact that you are separating doesn't protect them. Instead, if they think that their parents lie and aren't to be trusted, it may drive them away.

- Do allow children opportunities to talk about how they feel and be aware that mood and behaviour changes may be their reaction to the situation.

- Do encourage and help your children to be in frequent contact with their other parent through visits or by phone, post, email or text. It will be reassuring for them.

Listening and talking to your children when you're splitting up

Sometimes it is not easy to get your child to speak about what they are feeling. If your child bottles up their feelings they may get angry or have mood swings. They can find it difficult to tell you that they're upset or missing the other parent. Be patient and loving: it may take time for them to talk. Your child may want something that's not possible like you getting back together with your ex-partner. It's important that you explain to them why this can't happen. Remember – it's easier to help your child cope with being part of a separated family if you understand how they feel and what they need.

Stepfamilies

Following divorce and separation, one or both parents may be involved in a relationship with a new partner. Everyone will need time to adjust to this. For help with negotiating the changes this brings to your family you can contact Parentline Plus.

Questions children ask

Age 3–4

Your child asks: Why has my older sister got a different dad from me?

You could answer: When I was younger I didn't live with your dad; I had a different boyfriend then. I got pregnant and had your sister when I was with him. I love you both very much even though you have different dads.

Age 5–8

Your child asks: Why doesn't my best friend want to be my friend any more at school?

You could answer: Sometimes people don't want to be friends any more and we don't always know why. I'm not sure why your friend doesn't want to spend time with you, but I guess you are feeling sad about that. Would you like to tell me some more about what's been happening between you and your friend?

Note: the last question here gives you a chance to find out a bit more about this friendship, and how your child feels about it. This will give you a chance to listen and find out if there are any issues you may need to follow up with the school, such as bullying.

Age 9–13

Your child asks: My friend says boys will only be interested in me if I grow really big breasts, is that true?

You could answer: All girls grow breasts when they go through puberty – some grow bigger than others. This is quite normal – just as we have different sized hands or feet.

Some magazines make a lot of breast size and suggest that bigger is better but that's not true. You can feel good about yourself whatever your body shape.

Your body will change a lot during puberty. The way you look on the outside is only one part of what makes you attractive to other people. There are lots of other things like your personality and interests which make you the interesting person you are and far more attractive to boys than your breast size. So boys will be interested in you whatever your breast size.

Useful organisations

- Childline
- FFLAG
- Get connected
- www.itsnotyourfault.org.uk
- www.likeitis.org.uk
- Parentline Plus
- London Lesbian and Gay Switchboard
- Relate
- Sexwise
- Supportline
- www.there4me.com
- www.youngminds.org.uk

Sexuality

CHAPTER 6

What this chapter covers

- Sexuality, including lesbian, gay, bisexual and transgender sexuality.
- Sexual orientation.
- Homophobia and homophobic bullying.
- If your child identifies as lesbian, gay, bisexual or transgender.
- Supporting a young person to come out.

Sexuality

Before you talk with your child about sexuality, it could be useful to think about what it means to you. Sexuality is part of your personality and everyone has a sexuality. It's how you feel about yourself as a sexual being and how others see you. Your emotions, feelings, behaviour and culture all help to define your sexuality.

Sexuality develops throughout life, just like your body and your brain. It may take time to figure out who you are and what you want; even into later life. It's all part of the process of living.

The World Health Organization (WHO) has a broad definition of sexuality:

'Sexuality is a central aspect of being human throughout life and encompasses sex, gender identities and roles, sexual orientation, eroticism, pleasure, intimacy and reproduction. Sexuality is experienced and expressed in thoughts, fantasies, desires, beliefs, attitudes, values, behaviours, practices, roles and relationships.'[10]

Sexual orientation

Sexual orientation can take many forms – straight, gay, lesbian, bisexual. Even within these categories, everyone is different, some people's sexuality changes over time and some people aren't sure what their sexual orientation is.

Here are a few definitions:

Asexual
A person who doesn't feel sexual attraction or respond sexually to others.

Bisexual, or bi
A person sexually and emotionally attracted to both men and women (not necessarily at the same time).

Gender
Gender refers to the socially constructed roles, behaviours, activities and attributes that society considers appropriate for men and women. The terms male and female are sex categories, and the terms masculine and feminine are gender categories. Ideas about gender vary a lot between different societies.

Heterosexual (straight)
A person sexually and emotionally attracted to the opposite sex, that is, a man to women, or a woman to men.

Homosexual (gay and lesbian)
A person sexually and emotionally attracted to people of the same sex; gay is usually used for men attracted to other men, although sometimes for homosexual women as well; a lesbian is a woman attracted to other women.

Sex
The word 'sex' refers to the biological characteristics which define humans as female or male. It is also used to mean sexual activity.

(continued)

10 World Health Organization, 'Gender and reproductive rights', <http://www.who.int>, accessed 26 January 2007.

Transgender
People who have a strong feeling that their gender identity is not the same as the physical characteristics of the sex they are born with. Some people have gender reassignment, usually involving hormones and/or surgery.

Transsexual
A person who sees themself (and usually wants to become) another sex; transsexual people can be straight or gay.

Transvestite (cross dresser)
A person who chooses to wear any amount of clothing usually considered belonging to the opposite sex; this doesn't mean they are gay or straight or want to become another gender.

Talking with your child about sexuality

You can be open with your child from a young age about sexuality. Even small children notice adult relationships, and might ask questions about marriage, love, families and mums and dads.

You can bring your child up to understand that people can love who they want. Explain that some women love men, and some men love women; some men love men, some women love women, and some people love both. Help your child to understand that this is the way things are, and no sexual orientation is better or worse than another.

Tackling homophobia in your child

Homophobia is hating, abusing or bullying people because they are lesbian or gay. Children can pick up homophobic messages from a young age. For example, the word 'gay' is commonly used to mean stupid, weak or bad which in turn can help reinforce negative messages about homosexuality among children.

What would you do if...

Your nine-year-old daughter asks "what's a lesbian?"

Try and find out where your daughter heard the term. Children use and understand the words gay and lesbian far more than even ten years ago, due in part to greater openness in the media. Use this as an opportunity to explain what the words gay, lesbian, bisexual and straight mean, and how using them to insult someone is offensive. Explain that some women prefer to have relationships with women rather than men and that it is fine if they do. It is important that you let your daughter know that you would love and support her, whatever her sexual orientation.

Be aware of this, and also of any messages you might be giving your child without meaning to – most adults have absorbed some of the misunderstandings and assumptions that exist about lesbian, gay and bisexual people. If you hear your child using homophobic language, talk with them about it. Ask them why they are using it, and what they think it means. Help them to understand that using language like that can make some people feel very upset and isolated and that it's okay for someone to be lesbian, gay, bisexual or transgender. This doesn't mean that they are bad or weak; they just aren't heterosexual.

Avoid using homophobic language yourself, and let your child know that bullying someone, for any reason, is unacceptable.

Helping your child if they are at the receiving end of homophobic bullying

If your child is experiencing homophobic bullying, let them know you are there to support them. Reassure them that they do not deserve to be bullied, that what is happening to them is unacceptable and you will help to sort it out. Talk to them about whether they would like you to speak to the school. If they agree, contact their school and ask to speak to the head teacher or form teacher about what is happening.

Most schools have an anti-bullying policy, but very few of these deal specifically with homophobic bullying. If your child's school doesn't have a policy, flag up the 2007 guidance from the Department for Children, Schools and Families (DCSF) *Preventing and responding to homophobic bullying in schools*. This guidance provides school governors, teachers, heads and other staff with information on how to deal with homophobic bullying. You can find the guidance on www.stonewall.org.uk.

You can also find support from organisations such as FFLAG (Families and friends of lesbians and gays) and Stonewall.

If the bullying is happening outside school, you might be able to get help from the police. By law, homophobic bullying is considered a hate crime, and your child should not have to endure it.

If a young person identifies as lesbian, gay, bisexual or transgender

Many heterosexual parents assume their child will be heterosexual. It can be a shock to find out that their child feels they might be lesbian, gay, bisexual or transgender, and they might feel totally unprepared for dealing with it.

Try to consider what your reaction might be if your child was not heterosexual. How would you feel? How would you react when your child told you?

Many parents accept their child's sexuality – it is part of what makes their child unique and special – but others react with anger, disappointment, guilt (somehow feeling responsible for their child being 'different') or fear. They might feel they do not know their child, and can't relate to this new aspect of them. Bear in mind that a person cannot be 'turned' gay or straight. Your child's sexual orientation is not caused by anything you have done, and you cannot change the way they feel.

Remember, if a young person identifies as lesbian, gay, bisexual or transgender they are probably feeling isolated and scared. They might have known they are 'different' from their peers for months or years, and their own fear and confusion – particularly about your reaction – might mean they have taken a long time to find the courage to tell you.

Whatever your initial reaction, remember that your child needs your love and reassurance more than ever. They need to know that their sexual orientation doesn't affect your love for them.

Many parents find it easy to come to terms with their child's sexual orientation but for others it can be difficult and take a long time; it may help to remember that it has probably been the same for their child. You can acknowledge that it is difficult for you – the important thing is to reassure your child that you love them and are coming to terms with the news, even if it is gradually.

Many parents feel their child is going through a phase and will grow out of it. Whatever you might hope for in the future, remember that what your child is feeling right now is very real, and you should not insist that it is a phase.

"I was at work, and Donna my wife rang me in a distressed state; the cause for concern was our 14-year-old son Ben.

I rushed home not knowing what to expect. Was Ben in trouble at school? Had he been caught stealing? Taking drugs? I couldn't believe it was any of these. Not Ben. Not our quiet, well liked, well behaved 14-year-old son.

When I got home, the house was quiet. Donna and Ben were quiet. I could tell both had been crying. I sat down and Donna told me that Ben had told her that he was gay. I was glad I was sitting down! I was completely dumbfounded; I couldn't believe what I was hearing. Our 14-year-old son, gay? Not possible, just a phase, too young to know.

Ben had been spending a lot of time on his own upstairs on his computer. Donna had become suspicious and caught him on a gay chat line. After further questioning, Ben owned up to having been on gay chat lines for some time. He broke down in tears and came out to his mum. He told us how lonely he felt. We reassured him of how much we loved him and pledged our support for him.

The days that followed left Donna with mixed feeling. She felt ashamed to say that having Ben in the same room was sometimes like having an alien in our house, Donna admitted that she really didn't like Ben and she is glad to say that these feelings soon went away. We both went through a period of denial during which we questioned ourselves. What had we done wrong? Was it our fault? What could we have done to avoid it? But we didn't have any answers.

Contacting the Parents' Support Group was the best thing we ever did."

Reproduced with kind permission from www.fflag.org.uk

Supporting a young person to come out

Coming out (telling people that you are lesbian, gay, bisexual or transgender) is a very personal decision. It is an ongoing process, and a decision that lesbian, gay, bisexual and transgender people face throughout their life, whenever they meet new people. However, it is positive and empowering when the time is right.

If your child has come out to you, and has decided to come out to other people, you can support them. Let them know that it is their decision – they can decide who, when, how and where to tell people. There might be a local organisation or social group for young lesbian, gay, bisexual or transgender people; you could help your child find out. You could look in the phone book, at the library or ask at a local young people's service such as Brook or Connexions. Meeting with other young people who are going through the same experiences can be very important in helping young people overcome feelings of isolation.

Help your child understand that some people are scared of anything different, and can be ignorant about lesbian, gay, bisexual and transgender issues. This makes some people react badly when they find out somebody is not heterosexual. Reassure your child that is it perfectly healthy to be lesbian, gay, bisexual or transgender, and the problem does not lie with them – it lies with other people's ignorance.

There are organisations that can help you support your child in dealing with such reactions, such as FFLAG.

Questions children ask

Age 3–4

Your child asks: What does gay mean?

You could answer: When a man is gay it means that he loves men in the same way that men and women love each other.

Age 5–8

Your child asks: Why does my friend live with two mums instead of a mum and a dad?

You could answer: You, me and your mum are a family who love each other and live together (or describe your own family situation), but there are lots of different ways to be a family. Your friend lives with her two mums who love each other a lot, and they are a family too.

Age 9–13

Your child asks: What's a tranny?

You could answer: Tranny is a word that is used for a transsexual or transvestite. It can be used as a cruel word but that is because some people who use it may be frightened by people who are different from them.

A transsexual is a person who feels that they have been born into the wrong gender or sex. So, a woman feels as though she should really be a man, and a man feels as though he should really be a woman. Some people decide when they are fully grown to have an operation so they can physically change their male or female body parts, although not all transsexuals do this.

A transvestite is a person who sometimes chooses to wear clothes that the opposite gender usually wears. So, a woman might dress like a man, and a man might dress like a woman. Some people do it for pleasure and some people do it just because they feel more comfortable.

A transsexual and a transvestite might be lesbian, gay, straight or bisexual.

Useful organisations

- **fpa**
- Brook
- Connexions
- Department for Children, School and Families
- FFLAG (Families and friends of lesbians and gays)
- London Lesbian and Gay Switchboard
- Stonewall

Sex

CHAPTER 7

What this chapter covers

- Building your child's self-esteem so they are able to say no or negotiate condom use.
- The mechanics of sex.
- Safer sex.
- Pornography.
- Sex and the law.
- Sexual imagery in the media.

How you feel about your child growing up

It can feel like a challenge to accept that your child is developing into a sexual person, but try to remember that this is completely natural. You can help them by making sure they know what growing up is all about, and that what they are going through is normal.

If you find it very uncomfortable discussing sex and relationships with your child, don't just ignore the topic or hope they will muddle through by themselves. There are organisations that can offer help and support; don't be afraid to contact them (see Useful organisations at the end of this chapter).

> "My four-year-old son had a phase of asking about willies. What are willies for? Where's your willy mum? Why has daddy got a big willy? I explained that boys have willies and girls have a tuppence, which was the only word that came into my head. For a while he wanted to know if everybody had a willy, so we'd be in the supermarket and he'd be asking, 'does that man have a willy?'. It was fortunate that I kind of knew the man on the meat counter, and he knew I had small kids who ask questions at the most inappropriate times! So I just said, 'Yes, he does have a willy, but can we talk about this later because we're in public'. I just answered it and moved on, and he seemed fine with that."

Mother of two sons, aged four and 19 months, and a daughter, aged three

Teenage pregnancy

The UK has the highest teenage birth and abortion rates in Western Europe.

You can help your child avoid a teenage pregnancy by making sure they know how pregnancy happens, and how they can stop it from happening. By helping to develop their confidence in making decisions about their own behaviour, you'll give them the assertiveness to say no if they do not want to have sex, and the maturity to use contraception if they do.

Building your child's self-esteem as they get older

Giving your child plenty of love, affection and positive attention from a young age will help them know that they are loved and valued. Even if they don't want physical signs of affection, such as hugs, as they reach puberty, it is still important that they know you are there for them. Tell them you love them, and spend time with them. Show an interest in the things they like to do, and try not to be negative about them. Respect their decisions – within reason, of course; your child still needs to respect your rules too. See Chapter 4 for more about building self-esteem.

Puberty is a time when many young people want to become more independent from their parents, but this doesn't mean that they want to split from you entirely. Your love is still important to them, even if sometimes it doesn't feel like that.

Puberty is also a time when young people have to make a lot of decisions – about school, friends and social activities, as well as about boyfriends, girlfriends, sex and relationships. By building their knowledge and self-esteem, you can help them feel more confident in making the decisions they feel are right. Don't let sex be a hidden issue that your son or daughter can't talk about; they need to be able to talk about it in order to assert themselves, and to withstand any pressure someone might put on them.

When it comes to sex, it is important to talk with young people about the things they need to think about before they have sex. Let them know:

- It is their choice to have sex – it's an important decision and they shouldn't do it before they are ready.
- They should never feel they should have sex because someone is pressuring them to.
- They shouldn't pressure anyone else into having sex.
- If they have any doubts or think they might regret having sex, it's fine for them to wait.
- If they start having sex and want to stop, they have the right to change their mind.

Despite the number of teenage pregnancies in this country, and what young people may boast about to each other, most of them are not having sex. The average age when people first have sex is 16, but many people wait until they're older.[11] Let your son or daughter know that the following are not good reasons to have sex:

- My boyfriend/girlfriend says they'll leave me if I don't have sex.
- All my friends are having sex.
- I've had sex before, so I have to have it now.
- I want to find out how it feels/what it's like.

Reassure them that they don't need to make a decision based on what they've done in the past, or what they think their friends are doing. They need to make their own decision based on what they know is right for them. Remind them that a loving boyfriend/girlfriend respects how someone feels, and doesn't put pressure on them to do anything they don't want to do.

People often find that changing a relationship to a sexual one is a bigger step than they think. Let your son or daughter know that they don't have to 'go all the way' to have a good time.

The mechanics of sex

If you're going to be talking to your son or daughter about sex it's probably a good idea to brush up on some basic biology so you can pass on accurate information and answer any questions they might have.

---

11 Wellings K et al, 'Sexual behaviour in Britain: early heterosexual experience', *Lancet*, vol 358 (2001), 1843–1850.

What would you do if...

Your 16-year-old daughter tells you she has an appointment at the local sexual health clinic.

Whatever your reaction to this news try not to jump to conclusions – there could be several reasons why your daughter is going to the clinic. If you feel angry or upset talk to her when you're feeling calmer and try not to over react to the possibility that she is having sex. Because she has chosen to be quite open with you she may want to talk to you in more detail about why she is going but don't force her to tell you or push her for more information than she is comfortable giving. This could be a good opportunity to have a more general chat with your daughter about relationships and to ensure she is not feeling under pressure to have sex.

Whatever her reason for visiting the clinic and however you feel about it, it is important that you let your daughter know that you think she has acted responsibly. You could ask whether she is comfortable going to the clinic on her own and offer to go with her if she wishes, now or any time in the future.

In males

The penis contains erectile tissue which fills with blood when a man is sexually aroused. This causes an erection, making the penis longer and thicker.

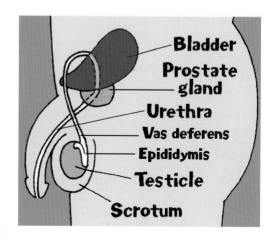

At ejaculation sperm passes along the sperm ducts and out of the body at the tip of the penis, through the urethra. On the way, fluid is added to the sperm, helping to nourish and transport them. This mixture of fluid and sperm is called semen. The average ejaculation contains up to 300 million sperm and will fill a teaspoon.

To prepare for ejaculation, a small amount of fluid, called pre-ejaculation fluid, is produced from the Cowper's glands. This fluid leaks out of the penis before ejaculation, and may contain sperm. This means a woman can get pregnant if a man withdraws his penis before ejaculating, as sperm may already have travelled into her body in the pre-ejaculation fluid.

When a man ejaculates, the muscles of the penis contract forcing the semen out of the penis in spurts. Straight after ejaculation the fluid is thick but it becomes more liquid after a few minutes; this helps to release the sperm.

In females

The vagina has glands which produce lubricating secretions when women are sexually aroused. This helps the penis enter the vagina (penetration). The vaginal walls are stretchy, allowing it to stretch around a penis during sex.

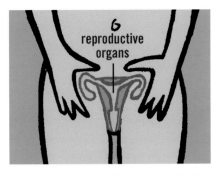

When a man ejaculates inside a woman's vagina, the sperm travel up through the cervix and into the uterus and fallopian tubes. Sperm wait for an egg to be released; they can live for up to seven days in a woman's uterus and fallopian tubes, and fertilise an egg.

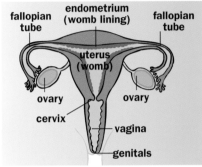

When the ovary releases an egg, small beating hairs and tiny wave-like contractions help the egg travel along the fallopian tube, where it may meet a sperm. The egg lives for up to 24 hours.

Only a small number of sperm will actually survive the trip to the fallopian tubes and finally only one sperm will actually enter the egg.

The sperm attaches itself to the egg and produces a special substance which dissolves the outer coat of the egg. Once it has entered, the egg coating is repaired, and no other sperm can get in.

Once the sperm is fully inside the egg (which takes about three hours), fertilisation has taken place.

The fertilised egg is wafted down the fallopian tube to the uterus. Here, it settles and over a few days attaches itself to the thick, nutritious lining. Implantation has now taken place, conception is complete and the pregnancy begins. The time from ovulation to implantation is around ten days.

"Out of the blue, my son – I think he was about nine – asked where the clitoris is. There was no build up to that whatsoever! My view is, if they're old enough to ask the question, they're old enough to get an answer. I told him straight it was part of a woman's body in her genital area. And that was it – 'eurgh!' and he was gone. One mention of the underneath parts and that was it. He'd obviously seen or heard it somewhere. My older son was there and he said to his brother, 'If you find where it is, girls will love you!'"

Mother of two daughters, aged seven and 12, and two sons, aged 15 and 28

Foreplay

Having sex doesn't just involve penetration. Foreplay is any sexual activity people do in the build-up to penetration.

Foreplay is part of sex, and can include kissing, touching, stroking, and exploring each other's bodies with hands, lips and tongue. Foreplay can take place as long as both partners want it to; it can be a very intimate and loving experience. It can be the time for partners to find out what they like, and what their partner likes.

Safer sex

Young people can help protect themselves against sexually transmitted infections by using a condom each time they have sex. For more information on safer sex see Chapter 8.

Oral sex

You might feel uncomfortable talking about oral sex with your child. But young people might hear about it from friends or on TV, and if they ask about it you need to give them the facts. There are risks with oral sex that young people need to know about.

Oral sex involves a person using their mouth, tongue and lips to stimulate:

- a woman's vagina, vulva and clitoris – known as cunnilingus, going down, giving head
- a man's penis – known as fellatio, blow job, going down, giving head
- a person's anus – known as rimming.

Many people give and receive oral sex as an enjoyable part of their sex life. There is no risk of pregnancy from having oral sex but some sexually transmitted infections can be passed on this way.

Some infections are spread more easily through oral sex than others. Oral sex is generally safer than unprotected (without a condom) vaginal or anal sex but there are ways of making oral sex safer.

The infections most commonly passed on through oral sex are:

- genital herpes
- gonorrhoea
- syphilis.

Infections less frequently passed on include chlamydia, HIV, hepatitis A, hepatitis B, hepatitis C and genital warts.

People can help protect themselves against infections during oral sex by using a condom on the penis, or a square piece of latex or polyurethane on the anus or female genitals (sometimes known as a dam). This acts as a barrier between the mouth and vagina or anus.

People should avoid oral sex if they or their partner:

- have a sexually transmitted infection
- have sores, cuts, ulcers, blisters, warts or rashes around the genitals, anus or mouth
- have any unhealed or inflamed piercings in the mouth or genitals
- have a throat infection.

Anal sex

Although you may feel uncomfortable talking about anal sex, young people will probably hear about it, and you need to be able to answer any questions they have.

Anal sex is when the penis penetrates the anus. Some people – male and female – enjoy anal sex as part of their sex life. There is no risk of pregnancy from anal sex, but sexually transmitted infections can be passed on this way.

Infections that can be passed on through unprotected (without a condom) anal sex include:

- HIV
- chlamydia
- syphilis
- genital herpes
- gonorrhoea
- genital warts.

People can help protect against sexually transmitted infections during anal sex by using a condom properly every time they have sex. The condom must be put on after the penis is erect and before there is any contact between the penis and the anus. See Chapter 9 for more information on sexually transmitted infections.

Sexual imagery in the media

There is a lot of sexual imagery in the media – on TV, in newspapers, music, magazines, adverts, the internet, computer games and films. Your child will be exposed to these, whether you want them to be or not. Sexual imagery is used to sell everything from chocolate to cars.

Images in the media can have a positive or negative effect on the sexual development of children and young people. For example, a music video might show women dancing in a sexually provocative way, wearing clothes that show much of their body. This can make young women feel they need to look and behave in a similar way in order to fit in; or it can make young men feel that women are there to be looked at only in terms of sex.

Sexual imagery can sometimes be violent. This makes it seem acceptable to young people to use words and actions that are offensive or abusive, and they may copy this behaviour.

On another level, the men and women used as models in the media are usually slim and conform to stereotypes of beauty, and this can have a negative effect on young people's self-esteem. It can be very confusing for young people to see all these images of models, sex and violence, and difficult for parents to counteract them.

You can help your child view these images more critically (and not feel they have to be like the people in these images) by building their self-esteem. You can tell your child that not everybody looks like a model, and there are many different ways of being beautiful. Have a look at the illustration on p78 and explain that models may have achieved that look through hours spent in the gym or plastic surgery and that images are often manipulated with faults airbrushed out. Tell them that although sex is an important part of life, it is not more important than loving and respecting people, or being happy with yourself as you are.

Let your child know that these sexual or violent images don't have to be seen as a desirable way to be and it is not acceptable to treat someone in an offensive or abusive way. Remind them that these images are not real life and that you don't have to be beautiful to have fun, love and be loved. For example, if you see a music video with sexualised imagery on TV, you can use it to start a discussion with your child and find out what they think about the clothes the people in the video are wearing and the way they are behaving. You could point out that the people are not behaving like that in real life; they are filming a video. You and your child could talk about the messages that this kind of sexualised behaviour sends out to other people.

Don't ignore sexual imagery in the media; your child will be exposed to it and your support in dealing with it is important.

Pornography

Young people will probably hear about, or see, pornography at some point. There is pornography for men and women – in magazines, films and on the internet. It is increasingly having a role and impact on young people's attitudes, self image, sexual behaviour, sexual negotiation and sexual relationships. Getting hold of often uncensored and unrestricted pornography is getting easier, particularly through the internet. Although there has not been a lot of research into it, it is possible that looking at pornography may influence young people's sexual attitudes and what they get up to sexually. There is also some concern from people working with young people that young people who look at pornography may be more likely to have issues relating to how they feel about themselves and unrealistic ideas about body image, and they may feel more pressure to perform certain types of sex such as anal sex and unsafe sex.

Pornography rarely shows condoms being used or discussions about whether both partners are happy with what they're doing.

How young men and women use pornography

Research has suggested that young men in particular use pornography to satisfy their curiosity about sex, sexual positions and female body parts.[12] They often turn to pornography because of the lack of clear pictures and open discussion in sex and

---

12 Wallmyr G and Welin C, 'Young people, pornography, and sexuality: sources and attitudes', *The Journal of School Nursing*, vol 22, no 5 (2006), 290–295.

relationships education. They are more likely to look at more pornography than young women and are more likely than women to choose hard-core material. Research has found that the majority of women have a negative attitude to pornography compared with men and most commonly describe it as being degrading.[13] However, some more recent research has shown that more women are now viewing pornography than ever before – on their own and in a couple to enhance sexual pleasure and intimacy.[14]

What would you do if...

You find a pile of your 18-year-old son's lads' mags in his 12-year-old brother's room. Also, your younger son has recently begun to make his bed instead of scattering his sheets in the morning as usual.

The last thing you want to do is embarrass your younger son. You probably suspect that he is masturbating, or having wet dreams, and trying to cover up the evidence. Maybe you've noticed the new attention he is giving to girls. This is all healthy and normal. It may be worth chatting to both your sons about the way men and women are portrayed in lads' mags. However, you need to be careful to make it clear that you came across the magazines in your son's room by accident and weren't prying.

You could talk about what makes someone sexy or attractive and work around to the idea that images of male and female models in magazines are highly idealised (and often airbrushed). They also usually present a very stereotyped image of men and women. Try and encourage your sons to be aware that in reality we all have a sexual side and that people of all ages, shapes and sizes can find each other sexually attractive. If you don't talk to your sons you may find that they are learning everything they know about sex and relationships from magazines.

Pornography can give a very distorted view of sex and what people's bodies look like. Make sure your son or daughter knows that it is not about emotions and that they should never:

- feel pressured to look at pornography
- make someone else look at pornography
- let anyone film or photograph them.

---

13 Rogala C and Tyden T 'Does pornography influence young women's sexual behaviour?' *Women's Health Issues*, vol 13, (2003), 39–43.

14 Paul P, *Pornified: How Pornography is Transforming our Lives, our Relationships, and our Families* (Times Books, 2005).

It is illegal to sell pornographic films to anyone who is under 18. However, newsagents can sell pornographic magazines to someone who is under 18 but many choose not to. Some kinds of pornography are always illegal, no matter what the age of the person looking at it, such as pornography involving children, animals and extreme violence.

Sex and the law

It is against the law for anyone to have sex with a young person under the age of 16. This is the same for young men and women and for heterosexual (straight) and homosexual (lesbian/gay) sex. This is known as the age of consent. Specific laws protect children under 13, who cannot legally give their consent to any form of sexual activity.

In reality, some young people under 16 will have sex. For some, simply saying it is not legal will not persuade them not to have sex. A better approach is to suggest they wait until they are ready and in a committed relationship. You could emphasise the risks of one-night stands or casual sex. If they are having sex it is important that they feel they can talk with you, if they wish to, and that they know about safer sex.

Alcohol and drugs

Some young people experiment with alcohol and/or drugs. This book is not about the effects and risks of drinking or using drugs, but they are worth mentioning here.

Being drunk or under the influence of drugs can affect a person's ability to make decisions and to look after themselves, or even make them incapable of walking, talking, asserting themselves (for example, saying no) or getting home safely. This can leave people vulnerable to unsafe sex, or sexual assault.

Make sure that your son or daughter knows the importance of making decisions about their own safety – and that being drunk or taking drugs can prevent them making sensible decisions. Tell them that even if drugs make them feel sexy and sexually confident and sex seems like a great idea when they're out of it, the risks they could be taking when they're not in control could put them in danger. In a survey one-third of 15–19-year-old girls and more than one-quarter of boys regretted having sex that happened when they'd been drinking.[15] Make sure your child knows the basics of personal safety. You will find lots of information in Chapter 11.

For more information and support on drugs and alcohol, and what to do if you think your child might have a problem, contact Frank – the drugs information organisation – or Alcohol Concern.

Questions children ask

Age 3–4

Your child asks: Mum, where's your willy?

You could answer: I don't have a willy because only boys and men have willies. Women and girls have vaginas, which are inside.

Age 5–8

Your child asks: My friend told me that a baby is made when a daddy puts his willy in a mummy's belly button. Is that right?

You could answer: No, that's not quite right. Babies are made when a mummy and daddy love each other and are feeling sexy. When they both want to, they have special cuddles when the daddy puts his penis into the mummy's vagina.

Age 9–13

Your child asks: What's oral sex?

This means using your mouth or tongue to lick or suck the sexual parts on a man or woman's body to give them sexual pleasure. Sometimes adults do this, when they both want to.

---

15 Ingham R, Survey commissioned by Channel 4 for the series *Generation Sex*, presented 16 October 2001.

fpa ᘻ Speakeasy: Talking with your chidren about growing up

Useful organisations

- **fpa**
- Alcohol Concern
- Brook
- www.condomessentialwear.co.uk
- Frank
- www.likeitis.org
- Sexwise

Contraction

CHAPTER 8

What this chapter covers

- The different methods of contraception available.
- How they work.
- Their advantages and disadvantages.
- Where to get them.

Contraception enables people to prevent pregnancy, and to decide when, or if, to have a baby. All contraceptive methods (apart from male condoms and male sterilisation) are used by women, and because of this, some people think that contraception is a woman's responsibility. But it is as much a man's responsibility as a woman's.

This chapter explains the various methods of contraception available, how they work, their advantages and disadvantages, and where young people can get them. Young men and women need to know about the different methods of contraception that are available.

No method of contraception is 100 per cent effective, but if used correctly the methods listed below are effective in preventing pregnancy.

Young people, including those under 16, can get free information and help about contraception from:

- a contraception clinic or sexual health clinic

- a young people's service

- a general practice, unless they say they don't provide contraception services

- some genitourinary medicine (GUM) clinics.

Where to find out about contraception services:

- You can find out about all sexual health services, including young people's services, from **sexual health direct**, run by **fpa**, on 0845 122 8690 or at www.fpa.org.uk.

- You can find details of general practices and pharmacies in England at www.nhsdirect.nhs.uk and in Wales at www.wales.nhs.uk. In Scotland you can find details of general practices at www.show.scot.nhs.uk. In England and Wales you can also call NHS Direct on 0845 46 47 and in Scotland NHS 24 on 0845 4 24 24 24. In Northern Ireland call **fpa**'s helpline on 0845 122 8687 or for details of general practices see www.n-i.nhs.uk.

- You can also get details of your nearest contraception, genitourinary medicine (GUM) or sexual health clinic from a telephone directory, health centre, local pharmacy, hospital, midwife, health visitor or advice centre.

- You can find details of GUM or sexual health clinics from the Sexual Health Line on 0800 567 123 or at www.condomessentialwear.co.uk.

- You can find details of young people's services from Brook on 0800 0185 023 or from Sexwise on 0800 28 29 30, or at www.ruthinking.co.uk.

Young people of any age can get advice, and clinics usually run special sessions for young people.

Confidentiality

All services are confidential, which means they won't tell anyone else a young person has used them. However, they may need to involve other services if they believe the young person, or someone else, to be at risk of harm (such as physical or sexual abuse). They will discuss this with the young person. Young people won't need to give their address.

Some facts about avoiding pregnancy

A woman can still get pregnant:

- if it is the first time she has sex
- if she does not have an orgasm
- if a man pulls out of her vagina before he comes
- if she has sex when she has a period
- if she douches (squirts fluid into the vagina). This can be harmful to women
- whatever position the couple has sex in.

What would you do if...

You find a condom in your 15-year-old child's bedroom when you're tidying up.

Don't jump to conclusions about why your son or daughter has a condom in their room. Maybe they were given it as part of sex and relationships education at school, or as a joke by friends. It doesn't necessarily mean that your child is having sex.

At this age children are very sensitive about their privacy so you must be careful to make it clear that you found the condom when you were tidying up. This may be an opportunity to ask your son or daughter how they are feeling about any relationship they are in at the moment and gently check with them if they are feeling pressured to have sex. Try to have a more general discussion about how they feel about themselves rather than focusing on the condom. It would be easy to alienate your son or daughter by over reacting to the possibility that they are having sex, even though you may be very concerned. It is important to reassure them that if they ever want to talk about a relationship or are thinking about having sex, they can always talk to you and come to you for support.

If your son or daughter is having sex, you should acknowledge their responsible behaviour in using condoms. This is also a good opportunity to find out if they know how to use a condom and fill in any gaps in their knowledge. It is important that they protect themselves from unwanted pregnancy and sexually transmitted infections so you need to make sure they know how to use condoms effectively. Tell them they can get confidential advice about contraception and sexually transmitted infections from young people's services. They can get details from Brook, Sexwise or at www.ruthinking.co.uk. fpa's helpline can also answer questions, discuss concerns, and help you and your child find the nearest clinic.

Methods of contraception are divided into two types and the table on pages 88–89 tells you more about them.

No user failure – these do not depend on remembering to take or use contraception.

User failure – these are methods the user has to use and think about regularly or each time they have sex. For these methods to be effective they must be used according to the instructions.

Emergency contraception

If a woman has had sex without using contraception or thinks her method might have failed there are two emergency methods she can use to prevent pregnancy:

- **The emergency hormonal pill** (not to be confused with the combined pill) – must be taken up to three days (72 hours) after sex. It is more effective the earlier it is taken after sex.

- **An IUD** – must be fitted up to five days after sex, or up to five days after the earliest time she could have released an egg (ovulation).

Women can ask their doctor or nurse about getting emergency pills in advance, just in case they need them.

What would you do if...

One evening your 17-year-old daughter tells you that she is worried because she had sex with her boyfriend the day before and they did not use any protection as it just happened and was not planned.

Try to keep calm – even though you might feel shocked or angry, remember that your daughter is probably worried and she has had the courage to come to you for help. You could suggest getting emergency contraception to prevent her becoming pregnant, as well as getting tested for sexually transmitted infections. You could look together at fpa's information about emergency contraception at www.fpa.org.uk.

You could offer to go with your daughter to a nearby pharmacy that is open late in the evening to buy the emergency pill. Even if she prefers to go on her own, you could make sure she understands the instructions. You could also offer to go with her to the sexual health clinic so she can get tested for sexually transmitted infections, and get some advice about choosing a method of contraception. You could tell her that you are really glad she spoke to you, even though some things might feel embarrassing to talk about, and that if she has any worries like this in the future you would be happy to listen to her.

Contraceptive methods with no user failure

	Contraceptive injection	Implant
What is it?	• An injection of progestogen.	• A small, flexible rod put under the skin of the upper arm releases progestogen.
Effectiveness	• Over 99%.	• Over 99%.
Advantage	• Lasts for eight or 12 weeks – you don't have to think about contraception during this time.	• Works for three years but can be taken out sooner.
Disadvantage	• Can't be removed from the body so side effects may continue while it works and for some time afterwards.	• It requires a small procedure to fit and remove it.

Contraceptive methods with user failure

  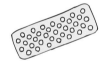

	Contraceptive vaginal ring	Contraceptive patch	Combined pill (COC)	Progestogen-only pill (POP)
What is it?	• A small, flexible, plastic ring put into the vagina releases estrogen and progestogen.	• A small patch stuck to the skin releases estrogen and progestogen.	• A pill containing estrogen and progestogen, taken orally.	• A pill containing progestogen, taken orally.
	Effective only if used according to instructions …		Effective only if used according to instructions …	
Effectiveness	• Over 99%.	• Over 99%.	• Over 99%.	• 99%.
Advantage	• One ring stays in for three weeks – you don't have to think about contraception every day.	• Can make bleeds regular, lighter and less painful.	• Often reduces bleeding, period pain and pre-menstrual symptoms.	• Can be used by women who smoke and are over 35, or those who are breastfeeding.
Disadvantage	• You must be comfortable with inserting and removing it.	• May be seen and can cause skin irritation.	• Missing pills, vomiting or severe diarrhoea can make it less effective.	• Late pills, vomiting or severe diarrhoea can make it less effective.

Contraceptive methods with no user failure

 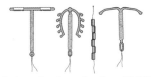

Intrauterine system (IUS)

- A small, T-shaped, progestogen-releasing, plastic device is put into the uterus.

- Over 99%.

- Works for five years but can be taken out sooner. Periods usually become lighter, shorter and less painful.

- Irregular bleeding or spotting is common in the first six months.

Intrauterine device (IUD)

- A small plastic and copper device is put into the uterus.

- Over 99%.

- Can stay in 5–10 years depending on type but can be taken out sooner.

- Periods may be heavier, longer or more painful.

Female and male sterilisation

- The fallopian tubes in women or the tubes carrying sperm in men (vas deferens) are cut, sealed or blocked.

- Overall failure rate of female sterilisation is one in 200, and one in 2,000 for male sterilisation.

- Sterilisation is permanent with no long or short-term serious side effects.

- Should not be chosen if in any doubt about having children in the future.

Contraceptive methods with user failure

Male condom

- A very thin latex (rubber) or polyurethane (plastic) sheath that is put over the erect penis.

Female condom

- Soft, thin polyurethane sheath that loosely lines the vagina and covers the area just outside.

Diaphragm/cap with spermicide

- A flexible latex (rubber) or silicone device, used with spermicide, is put into the vagina to cover the cervix.

Natural family planning

- Fertile and infertile times of the menstrual cycle are identified by noting different fertility indicators.

Effective only if used according to instructions ... Effective only if used according to instructions ...

- 98%.

- 95%.

- Latex types are 92–96% effective. Silicone caps are less effective.

- If used according to teaching, up to 99% effective.

Condoms are the best way to help protect yourself against sexually transmitted infections.

- May protect against some sexually transmitted infections and cervical cancer.

- No chemicals or physical products means no physical side effects.

- May slip off or split if not used correctly or if wrong size or shape.

- Not as widely available as male condoms.

- Putting it in can interrupt sex. If you have sex again extra spermicide is needed.

- Need to avoid sex or use a condom at fertile times of the cycle.

Safer sex

Safer sex is when people take precautions against sexually transmitted infections and pregnancy. Using a condom properly every time you have sex will help protect against both. See below for more information about how to use condoms correctly.

Diaphragms and caps may offer some protection against sexually transmitted infections.

All other methods of contraception will help protect against pregnancy, but won't protect against sexually transmitted infections.

See Chapter 9 for more information on sexually transmitted infections.

More about using a condom

"My teenage son was going on holiday with a group of friends for the first time and I decided to raise the issue of condoms and keeping safe. The subject came up quite naturally in the end. We were going through the toiletries he needed to pack. I said something like 'While we're on the subject, do you think it might be good to pack some of these?' and gave him some condoms. The laughter broke the ice and led on to what was a good conversation – man-to-man you might say – about sex, and how important it is to protect yourself from infection as well as the whole question of unwanted pregnancy. I think he appreciated that it was me as his dad and not his mum that was having this conversation!"

Father of a son, 16

Most problems with condoms happen because people make mistakes using them:

● Condoms can be used on their own. They do not need to be used with spermicide.

● Be careful how you take the condom out of the packet – sharp fingernails and jewellery can tear the condom.

● To provide the best protection, a condom must be put on the penis when it is erect and before there is any contact between each other's genitals. This is because pre-ejaculation fluid and vaginal secretions may both pass on sexually transmitted infections, and pre-ejaculation fluid may contain sperm.

● Find the teat or closed end of the condom and gently squeeze it to get rid of air. This will also help you to roll it on the right way round.

● Still holding the end, roll the condom all the way down the penis.

● If it won't go to the base then it's probably inside out. If so, start again with a new condom as sperm could now be on the first one.

● As soon as the man has ejaculated and before the penis has had time to go soft, hold the condom firmly in place while withdrawing. Do this slowly and carefully so no semen is spilt.

● Condoms should be wrapped up and put in a bin, not down the toilet.

● If you have sex again, use a new condom.

Help young people negotiate using contraception

By making sure young people know how to use a condom, you are building their ability to make informed decisions about their health. You can also encourage them to think about how they could respond if their boyfriend/girlfriend makes excuses for not using contraception. For example:

Excuse:
My parents might find out I'm having sex.

Response:
They'll definitely find out you're having sex if I/you get pregnant – you can't hide something like that. And they might be happy to know you're using contraception; I'm sure they'd rather you were sensible and looking after yourself than taking risks that might affect your whole life.

Excuse:
Contraception spoils the romantic mood.

Response:
I won't be able to relax and enjoy sex with you if I'm worrying about pregnancy and babies or sexually transmitted infections. Lots of contraceptive methods don't interfere with sex at all – we can find out together about different methods if you like.

Excuse:
I'll stick by you if you get pregnant, so it doesn't matter.

Response:
You might believe that right now, but imagine if I got pregnant and we had a baby – you'd be a dad.
Having a baby is really hard work and puts a big strain on a relationship; I'm not ready for that.

Excuse:
Condoms take all the pleasure away.

Response:
No they don't – some kinds are really sensitive and there are lots of different types to try ... we can make it fun.
And besides, if you don't use a condom we won't be having sex so there won't be any pleasure at all.

Excuse:
It won't matter if I get pregnant, a baby will be someone to love.

Response:
But we're young – we'll never be teenagers again.
Being a parent will last forever, not just when the baby's born, and it's really hard work. You can have a baby in the future; I'm not ready for it now.

Questions children ask

Age 3–4

Your child finds a condom in the bathroom and asks: "What's this?".

You could answer: It's not a toy/sweet. These are special things that mummy and daddy use.

Age 5–8

Your child asks: What's a condom?

You could answer: Mummy and daddy use it to help stop them having another baby at the moment.

If they want more information you could explain: A condom is something that is often made of thin rubber. You roll it down a man's penis before he has sex and when sperm comes out of his penis it stays in the condom. If he is having sex with a woman then it means that it protects her from getting pregnant. It can also help protect against passing on infections while people are having sex.

Age 9–13

Your child asks: What's the pill?

You could answer: The pill is something women can take if they do not want to have a child at the moment. It is like a medicine that stops women releasing an egg every month and this means that she does not get pregnant if she has sex with her partner.

Useful organisations

- **fpa**
- Brook
- www.condomessentialwear.co.uk
- Sexwise

Sexually transmitted infections

What this chapter covers

- Sexually transmitted infections.
- Signs and symptoms.
- Where people can go to get advice, tests and treatment.
- Safer sex.

However you might feel about young people having sex, the fact is that if they *are* having sex, they need to know how to look after their health. You can help by making sure they know what the risks are, and where they can go for help. If you tell them this within the context of your own values and beliefs, they will know how you feel about it but they will still feel able to make their own decisions.

A person doesn't need a lot of sexual partners to get a sexually transmitted infection. Anybody who has sex – male, female, straight, gay, lesbian, bisexual – can get one.

There are more than 25 sexually transmitted infections. Some of the most common are:

- chlamydia
- genital warts
- genital herpes
- gonorrhoea
- non-specific urethritis.

Less common, but not rare, ones are:

- trichomonas vaginalis
- pubic lice
- scabies
- hepatitis B
- syphilis
- HIV.

What is a sexually transmitted infection?

Some infections can pass to another person through unprotected vaginal, anal or oral sex and through sharing sex toys. Infections spread in this way are known as sexually transmitted infections.

Safer sex

Young people can help protect themselves against sexually transmitted infections by using a condom each time they have sex. For more information on safer sex see Chapter 8.

Can they be treated?

Most sexually transmitted infections can be treated and it is usually best if treatment is started as soon as possible. Some viruses, such as HIV, never leave the body but there are drugs available that can reduce the symptoms and help prevent or delay the development of complications. If left untreated, many sexually transmitted infections can be painful or uncomfortable, and can permanently damage health and fertility, and can be passed on to someone else.

What would you do if...

Your 16-year-old son confides in you that he had unprotected sex with his new girlfriend and is worried that he has a sexually transmitted infection.

Try not to get angry; your son is worried and has come to you for help. How you react could affect whether or not he comes to you for help in the future. You could ask him why he is worried he has a sexually transmitted infection – does he have symptoms, or has his girlfriend told him she has one? Tell him the best thing to do is go to the sexual health clinic. Call **fpa's** helpline to find out where the local clinic is. You could offer to go with him.

Remind him that condoms will help protect against pregnancy and sexually transmitted infections and if he uses them properly he won't have to worry that he's got an infection. Tell him that clinics give out free condoms, and suggest he asks for some.

Let him know that you are glad he came to you, and he can always talk with you about anything that is troubling him, or if he needs advice. Tell him that if you don't know the answer to anything, you will try and find it out.

What are the signs and symptoms of a sexually transmitted infection?

Not everyone who has a sexually transmitted infection has signs and symptoms. Sometimes these don't appear for weeks or months and sometimes they go away, but you can still have the infection and pass it on to someone else. If someone has any of the following they should seek advice:

- unusual discharge from the vagina
- discharge from the penis
- pain or burning when passing urine
- itches, rashes, lumps, sores or blisters around the genitals or anus
- pain and/or bleeding during sex
- bleeding between periods (including women who are using hormonal contraception)
- bleeding after sex
- pain in the testicles or lower abdomen.

Even if someone doesn't have any signs and symptoms they may wish to seek advice or have a check-up, particularly if:

- they have had unprotected sex with a new partner recently
- they have had sex with other people without using a condom, or they know that their boyfriend/girlfriend has
- their boyfriend/girlfriend has a sexually transmitted infection
- they want to have a baby but they may have been at risk of infection.

Where can young people go if they are worried they might have an infection?

They can get all tests and treatments at a genitourinary medicine (GUM) or sexual health clinic. General practices, contraception clinics, young people's services and some pharmacies may also provide testing for some infections. If they can't provide testing, they will be able to give details of the nearest service that can.

All advice, information and tests are free. In England, Scotland and Northern Ireland prescriptions are free for under 16s and for 16–18-year-olds in full-time education. In Wales prescriptions are free for everyone.

What are the tests for sexually transmitted infections?

Tests for both men and women may include:

- An examination of the genitals, mouth, anus, rectum (back passage) and skin to look for obvious signs of infection.
- Testing a sample of urine.
- Having blood taken.
- Taking swabs from the urethra (tube where you urinate) and any sores or blisters.
- Taking swabs from the throat and the rectum. This is less common.

In women the tests might also include:

- Taking swabs from the vagina and cervix (entrance to the uterus).
- Having an internal examination.

What will a young person be tested for?

A young person will not automatically be tested for all infections. All tests are optional and should only be done with a young person's permission. Sometimes the results will be available straightaway, and sometimes there will be a wait. The service will explain how they will get the results.

Young people can also get information about sexually transmitted infections from **fpa** and the Sexual Health Line (see Chapter 13: Useful organisations).

Questions children ask

Age 3-4

It is unlikely that a child of this age would ask a question about a sexually transmitted infection.

Age 5-8

Your child says: A boy at school said I've got lice because I've been sexy with someone.

You could answer: You have head lice which walked from someone else's hair into your hair. There are lice that people can get when they are being sexy with each other but you don't have those.

Age 9-13

Your child asks: Someone at school said because my uncle is gay it means he has HIV. Is that true?

You could answer: Some people think that because someone is gay it automatically means that they have HIV, but it's not true. They probably think that just because they feel a bit frightened of gay men, or frightened of anything different. HIV is an infection that can be transmitted when people have sex if one person is already infected. It can affect anyone, gay and straight. The best way to try to make sure you don't get HIV is to use a condom correctly when you are having sex when you are older. You can't get HIV from being friends with someone.

Useful organisations

- **fpa**
- Brook
- www.condomessentialwear.co.uk
- Sexual Health Line
- Sexwise
- Terrence Higgins Trust

CHAPTER 10

Pregnancy choices

What this chapter covers

- Pregnancy choices available if your daughter is pregnant and isn't sure she wants to be, including continuing with the pregnancy, adoption and abortion.

- Where to go for help and support if your daughter is pregnant, or your son's girlfriend is pregnant.

Most of this chapter is written for parents of young women who are pregnant, but the sources of help and support can also help parents whose son's girlfriend is pregnant.

Your reaction

It might feel like a topic you don't even want to consider – your daughter getting pregnant, or your son's girlfriend becoming pregnant. But it does happen.

You can help young people avoid unplanned pregnancy by teaching them how pregnancy happens and how to use contraception, and giving them the confidence to decide to delay sex if they want to.

But if a pregnancy does happen, you need to know how to help your son or daughter get the help and support they need. It may be that the topic of unplanned pregnancy comes up when it doesn't involve your child – perhaps someone at school is pregnant, or there is a storyline on a TV programme. This can be a good opportunity to educate your child about pregnancy choices.

Abortion can feel like a difficult topic to talk about, but it doesn't have to be. In the simplest terms, abortion is a way a woman can end a pregnancy that she doesn't want. Abortion is legal in the UK (although extremely difficult to obtain in Northern Ireland), and your child will become aware of it at some stage so if you make sure they have accurate facts about abortion you will help ensure your child is not confused by half-truths or myths.

Helping your daughter if she has an unplanned pregnancy

If your daughter has an unplanned pregnancy, your first reaction may vary. Some parents might feel disbelief and anger and that she has ruined her life. If this is how you feel, try not to take these feelings out on her. She might be feeling very isolated and frightened, and your reaction could be the thing she is most anxious about. Your daughter does not want to disappoint you, and will be worried.

Some parents might feel pleased at the thought of their daughter having a baby, and welcome the news about her pregnancy.

Whatever your own reaction, remember that you cannot assume your daughter will be feeling the same as you. She could be feeling anxious and scared, or excited and happy, or a mixture of these things. What she needs is for you to listen to how she is feeling about the pregnancy, and to offer your help and support in whatever decision she makes.

If your son's girlfriend is pregnant

If your son's girlfriend is pregnant he will be going through a range of emotions too – he might feel frightened, ashamed, disappointed or as though he has ruined his life. On the other hand, he might feel glad that his sperm is 'working', excited at such a big event in his life, or happy at the prospect of becoming a dad. He might feel a mixture of all these things.

What he needs from you at this time is your support. If you feel angry, upset or disappointed, try not to take this out on him. Let him know you love him, and that you are there if he needs you.

Remind your son that if a young woman is pregnant, it is her decision whether to continue with the pregnancy and keep the baby, have the baby adopted, or end the pregnancy by having an abortion. The father of the baby has no legal say in the decision. Many young women do consult the father of the child and come to a joint decision, but they don't have to. Where partners have tried to prevent an abortion by legal action they have failed.

If your son is finding the situation very difficult, he can contact an organisation that offers support to young people, such as Brook or Sexwise.

Whether your daughter is pregnant or your son's girlfriend is pregnant, it is important that you reassure them that you love them and are there for them. Let your daughter know you are there to help her make the decision that is right for her and that you can work through this together; it is not the end of the world, even though it may feel like it right now. If your daughter feels positive about the pregnancy and wants to have the baby, she needs your support, however you might be feeling about it.

Make sure

The first thing your daughter should do is confirm the pregnancy. Pregnancy tests bought at the pharmacy are reliable, or you can get a test at a general practice, young people's service or a contraception, sexual health or genitourinary medicine (GUM) clinic. Some NHS walk-in centres offer them too.

The earliest time a woman can do a pregnancy test is the day her period is due. If she doesn't know when her period is due, the earliest she can do a test is 21 days after unprotected sex. Tests done before this may not pick up on the pregnancy.

A positive test

A positive test means that your daughter is definitely pregnant. However she feels about the pregnancy, she needs to think about what to do. It is important she takes time to make the decision that is right for her, but it is also important not to delay the decision.

Do not pressure her into doing something she doesn't want to do, however strongly you might feel about it. The decision is hers. She can choose to:

I don't want a child until I've finished my education.

- continue with the pregnancy and keep the baby
- end the pregnancy by having an abortion
- continue with the pregnancy and have the baby adopted.

Making the decision

It is essential that your daughter is given accurate information and time to explore how she feels, so she can make the decision that is right for her.

As well as talking with family or friends, if this is what she wants to do, there are also other services that offer support.

The following services can talk confidentially and for free about the pregnancy and her options:

- her general practice (GP or nurse)
- a contraception or sexual health service
- a young people's service or Brook clinic
- **fpa**'s helpline. Women who live in Northern Ireland can also contact **fpa**'s unplanned pregnancy counselling service. This service is free and can offer non-judgmental and non-directive counselling and information on all the options to help your daughter decide what to do.

Marie Stopes and bpas can also talk about pregnancy choices with young women – there will be a charge for this service.

Be aware that some organisations may not offer unbiased pregnancy counselling or advice and may lead women into making the wrong choice for them.

Things to think about

When your daughter is making her decision about the pregnancy, let her know it can be helpful to consider the following things:

Her life now.
What is the most important thing in her life? This could involve family, friends, work and education.

Her future.
What are her hopes and aims for the future?

How would these things be affected if she decided to:

- continue with the pregnancy and keep the baby
- end the pregnancy by having an abortion
- continue with the pregnancy and have the baby adopted.

If your son's girlfriend is pregnant, he can think about these things too, although he will not have a say in the decision about whether or not she continues with the pregnancy.

Another way for your daughter to think about her situation is to consider how the statements below make her feel:

- I feel ready to be a parent and bring up a child.

- I don't want to be pregnant.

- Having a baby will stop me doing the things in my life that are most important to me.

- I do want to have a baby one day but I'd rather wait (because I feel I'm too young, or I'd like to be in a committed relationship).

- I am willing to give up other things in my life in order to bring up a child.

- My family would help me if I have a baby.

- My family wouldn't approve if I have a baby.

- My partner wants to have a baby with me.

- I couldn't go through with an abortion.

- I agree with abortion.

- I wouldn't be able to give my baby away.

Continuing with the pregnancy

If your daughter decides to continue with the pregnancy, she needs to start her antenatal care (care during pregnancy) as soon as possible, whether she is planning to keep the baby or to have it adopted.

To start antenatal care, she can visit her general practice or register with one. In some areas, she might be able to go directly to a midwife at her nearest maternity unit.

The midwife or doctor will be able to talk with her about healthy eating, taking folic acid (a vitamin supplement), stopping smoking, cutting out (or down on) alcohol, getting advice and tests for sexually transmitted infections, and whether any medicines she is taking are unsafe during pregnancy.

Family or friends may react to news of a pregnancy in different and sometimes surprising ways. In our society, pregnancy and parenthood are matters of great public concern.

For a young person, making a pregnancy public may also be revealing for the first time that they have been sexually active. How accepting people are will vary depending on age and cultural or religious background.

Your daughter needs a lot of support, and she needs to know that she can depend on you. Reassure her that you love her, that you respect her decision, and you will help and support her in any way you can. There might be local groups for teenage parents, or antenatal classes specially for teenagers. Ask the midwife what is available.

If your son's girlfriend is pregnant encourage and support him to be involved with the pregnancy, where possible.

You and your daughter can find out more about pregnancy, parenthood, benefits and more at the following places:

- **fpa**
- National Childbirth Trust
- Working Families.

Abortion

Let your daughter know that legal abortion is a safe way of ending a pregnancy. This is a decision she might make because she does not want to be pregnant and have a baby at this time.

How easy it is to arrange an abortion can vary throughout the UK, and it can be extremely difficult to obtain an abortion in Northern Ireland.

Legal abortion is safer and easier the earlier it is done in pregnancy. The majority of abortions are carried out before 13 weeks, and most of the rest are carried out before 20 weeks. Abortion after 24 weeks is not common, but is legal in certain circumstances (for example, to save the woman's life or if there is a substantial risk of physical or mental disability if the baby was born).

If your daughter decides to have an abortion:

- She can go to her general practice, a contraception or sexual health service, or a young people's service. These places can refer her for an abortion through the NHS. It can be extremely difficult to get referred for an abortion in Northern Ireland. Girls and women in Northern Ireland can contact **fpa**'s unplanned pregnancy service. They will be able to advise on getting a private abortion in England, if this is what the woman decides to do.

- She can also directly contact organisations that provide abortion for a fee (outside Northern Ireland) – she does not have to be referred by another service. These include bpas, Marie Stopes, Calthorpe Clinic and South Manchester Private Clinic (see Chapter 13: Useful organisations).

What would you do if...

Your 16 year old daughter tells you that she is pregnant. She is very confused and does not know if she wants to have the baby or have an abortion.

Whatever your reaction to the news, try to remember that this is about your daughter, not you. If you feel angry, don't take it out on her; she is confused and has come to you for support. Try to keep calm, and ask her how she is feeling. Let her know you are there for her, and will support her whatever decision she makes.

It is important to find out for sure whether she is pregnant. Buy a test from a pharmacy for her to do at home, or go with her to your general practice, contraception or sexual health clinic or young people's service. If she is not pregnant, talk with her about the importance of contraception and using condoms to help protect against pregnancy and sexually transmitted infections, and offer to go with her to a contraception clinic to arrange contraception.

If she is pregnant, reassure her that you are there for her, and explore her options with her – continuing the pregnancy and keeping the baby, having the baby adopted, or ending the pregnancy with an abortion. See the sections in this chapter on Making a decision and Things to think about for more detailed advice and organisations to contact for support. She needs to take time to make the decision that is right for her, but she also needs to make up her mind as soon as possible so that she can start antenatal (pregnancy) care or get an appointment for an abortion referral.

If she decides to continue with the pregnancy or have an abortion, she needs to make an appointment with her general practice as soon as possible. If you want to pay for an abortion privately, you can contact an organisation such as Marie Stopes or bpas.

Confidentiality

Any young woman who has an abortion, whatever age she is, has a right for that information to remain confidential. Her doctor, her parents and the father of the child do not have to know.

If your daughter is under 16 or has learning disabilities, it is possible for her to have an abortion without telling you. This is a difficult fact for many parents to accept, but try to remember that the law is there to help and protect children. Your daughter may be able to come and talk with you if she needs help, but there are young people who cannot talk with their parents. The doctors will encourage a young woman under 16 to involve her parent or carer, or another supportive adult, but if she chooses not to, she can still have an abortion if the doctors believe that she fully understands what is involved and it is in her best interests.

However, health professionals are obliged, with the young person's knowledge, to involve social services if they suspect her, or another person, to be at significant risk of harm (for example, sexual abuse).

What is involved in an abortion?

For some young women, deciding whether or not to have an abortion is easier if they know how an abortion is carried out. There are different procedures, and the method used depends on how long she has been pregnant. You or your daughter can find out more about abortion procedures from:

- **fpa** – the helpline adviser will be able to talk about abortion, and send out **fpa**'s *Abortion* booklet, or you can read about abortion on www.fpa.org.uk .
- The Royal College of Obstetricians and Gynaecologists' website, www.rcog.org.uk – this has clear information about abortion.

Supporting young people after an abortion

If your daughter has had an abortion, she might feel relief, anger, regret, guilt or sadness. These emotions may come and go, and might be heightened by sudden hormonal changes after an abortion.

For many young women, the emotional turmoil disappears rapidly. For others, it lingers. Allow your daughter to go through all these feelings; make sure she knows you are there, and that she has your love and support.

Your daughter can see a counsellor at the clinic where she had an abortion. She can do this even if it's a long time since the abortion. **fpa** in Northern Ireland also offers a counselling service for women who have had an abortion.

If your son's girlfriend has had an abortion he might have his own feelings of sadness or regret. Be there to talk with him and support him if he needs it. He can also talk with his GP or a counsellor if he wants to.

Adoption

Adoption could be an option if your daughter does not want to bring up the baby herself, but does not want an abortion.

Adoption is a way of giving the baby new parents who will bring him or her up as their own. Your child will continue with the pregnancy and give birth, but she won't look after the baby, and won't have legal rights or responsibilities regarding the child once the adoption is complete. The adoption isn't completed until after the baby is born, and after the adoptive parents have been granted an adoption order by the courts.

Your daughter can change her mind at any stage before the adoption order is granted, but it might not be easy (or even possible) to get the baby back, depending on how far the adoption has progressed. The court will make a decision based on what is best for the baby.

Giving up a baby for adoption can be a very difficult decision. If your daughter is considering it, she might find it helpful to talk with someone who can tell her more about adoption, including:

- the doctor or nurse at her general practice
- a social worker at the local hospital (contact the local hospital to find out whether there is a social worker attached to the maternity unit)
- an adoption social worker at the local authority's social services department or at a local voluntary adoption agency (contact the British Association for Adoption and Fostering).

The social worker or adoption agency will arrange special adoption counselling. This is to make sure that your daughter knows exactly what the adoption involves, and to explore all possible options with her to help her make the right decision for her.

They will be able to answer questions your daughter might have, including:

- Does the baby's father have a say in the adoption?
- Will I be able to help choose the adoptive parents?
- Will I be able to have any contact with the child once he or she is adopted?
- Can an adoption be undone if I want my baby back later?
- Will the baby be able to find me when he or she grows up?

If a mother wants to give a baby up for adoption but the father wants to bring up the baby himself, and they cannot come to an agreement about what to do, a court will have to decide whether it is in the child's best interests to be adopted or brought up by the father.

You can find more information in the adoption section at www.everychildmatters.gov.uk.

Contraception after pregnancy

Contraception may be the last thing on your daughter's mind after she has had a baby or an abortion, but it is something she needs to think about if she wants to avoid another pregnancy.

Many unplanned pregnancies happen in the first few months after childbirth, so even if she's not interested in sex at the moment, it is better to be prepared.

Your daughter will need to start using contraception immediately after an abortion, and three weeks after having a baby. It is possible to get pregnant two weeks after having an abortion and four weeks after having a baby. She should not wait for her periods to return, as it is possible to get pregnant before then (ovulation happens around two weeks before a period). All methods of contraception can be used straight after an abortion.

If your son's girlfriend was pregnant it is also important that you talk to him about contraception and make sure he knows how to use condoms correctly and where he can get them, so that he can help avoid another unplanned pregnancy in the future. This can also help him feel more in control of his own body.

See Chapter 8 for more information about where to get help and advice about contraception.

Questions children ask

Age 3–4

Your child asks: Why don't daddies have babies?

You could answer: Although it takes a mummy and a daddy to make babies, they only grow inside a special place in mummies' tummies. It is warm and comfortable in there and the baby can grow safely until it is big enough to come out on its own.

Age 5–8

Your child asks: Mum, how did the baby get in your tummy?

You could answer: When mums and dads love each other they cuddle very close, in a special grown-up way. Sometimes when they cuddle, a sperm travels from the dad's penis into the mum's vagina. It travels inside the mum until it meets a little egg. The sperm and the egg join together and a baby is made. This baby begins to grow inside a special place called a uterus; this is warm, comfortable and safe and allows the baby to grow bigger and bigger until it is big enough to come out.

Age 9–13

Your child asks: What's an abortion?

You could answer: An abortion is when a pregnancy is ended. It happens when an embryo or a fetus is taken out of the uterus, either by taking pills or by surgery. Sometimes a girl or woman gets pregnant but she doesn't want to have a baby, so she decides to have an abortion. It's a safe way of ending a pregnancy, and it doesn't mean she can't have a baby in the future if she wants one. If you ever find that you are pregnant, or get someone pregnant, please remember you can talk with me about it, and I will do all I can to help you. It's important for a woman to make up her mind as soon as possible, because an abortion is safer the earlier it is done, so don't put off thinking about it. Contraception methods are ways to prevent pregnancy happening in the first place, so it's important to know about these and use them if you have sex and don't want to get pregnant/your girlfriend to get pregnant.

Useful organisations

- **fpa**
- bpas
- British Association for Adoption and Fostering
- Brook
- Calthorpe Clinic
- www.condomessentialwear.co.uk
- www.eatwell.gov.uk
- Education for choice
- Every Child Matters
- Frank
- Go Smoke Free
- Marie Stopes
- National Childbirth Trust
- Royal College of Obstetricians and Gynaecologists
- Sexual Health Line
- Sexwise
- South Manchester Private Clinic
- Tommy's the Baby Charity

Keeping safe

CHAPTER 11

What this chapter covers

- Helping children stay safe.
- Safety advice for young people.
- Using the internet safely.
- Helping to protect young people from abuse.

Talking with your child about sex and relationships from an early age gives you the chance to let them know what is inappropriate adult behaviour towards children. They may be more likely to talk with you if they are concerned about the way an adult or young person is treating them.

Knowing what is inappropriate behaviour, and knowing where they can go for help or advice if they need it, means your child can keep as safe as possible from harm. Be aware that children can be at risk from adults they know and trust, including relatives, as well as from strangers.

Helping children stay safe

Help your child stay safe by making sure that they know:

- What is okay and what is not okay when an adult who is not their parent touches them.
- They can say 'stop' to an adult if the adult is touching them in a way they don't like.
- That they can always talk with you about anything that is bothering them.
- How to keep themselves safe on the internet – for more on internet safety, see later in this chapter.
- Not to go anywhere with someone they do not know, even if that person tells them that you have said it is okay. Tell your child that you will never ask a stranger to look after them, and that if an adult tells your child you have said this, then they are lying.
- They can make a noise, or shout for help. You might even want to teach your child a phrase they can shout, for example, 'help, call the police'.

Safety advice for young people

Young people of all ages need to know basic rules of keeping safe when they are out and about, including:

- Avoiding potentially dangerous or isolated areas, such as quiet pathways or underpasses.
- Not going anywhere with strangers, including getting into a car.
- Being aware of what is going on around them, and that listening to loud music on headphones will make them less aware.
- Keeping their mobile phone or wallet/purse hidden.
- Knowing a number they can call for help in an emergency, whether it is your number, your friend's number or the police.

Young people should:

- Tell someone where they're going and when they think they'll be back.
- Have credit on their phone and keep it charged.
- Work out how they're going to get home and keep aside enough money.
- Only use a licensed taxi firm and have the number with them.
- Be careful what they drink – drugs used to spike drinks can be colourless, odourless and tasteless.
- Avoid drinking too much alcohol, not accept drinks from strangers and keep their drink in sight.

If a young person feels odd, dizzy or wasted after a couple of drinks when normally they'd be okay, they need to:

- Go somewhere they feel safe.
- Get their friends to help them home (if they are out with friends).
- Get help from someone they can trust, or phone for help.

Suzy Lamplugh Trust provides lots of personal safety tips, and a special area for young people on their website, www.suzylamplugh.org.uk.

Help young people use the internet safely

The following information about internet safety is reproduced with kind permission from the National Society for the Prevention of Cruelty to Children (NSPCC).

Most children and young people go online for entertainment and to socialise. The internet offers great opportunities but children and young people must understand that the risks to their privacy and safety are real. It is important that you talk with your children about the possible dangers online regularly and make sure they feel they can talk to you if they are worried or concerned.

The dangers include

- Coming across disturbing information or images.

- Unwittingly opening or sharing files that can expose the family to internet thieves or virus software which damage, delete or copy data.

- Being bullied online when other users try to embarrass or intimidate them, or spread rumours or images about them.

- Sexual predators posing as children in the hope of befriending vulnerable children; including trying to persuade children to meet in person.

Guidelines

It is also a good idea to learn about the technology children use and to follow the guidelines below:

- Place the computer where the whole family can use it rather than out of sight in a bedroom.

- Use filtering software available to screen out some inappropriate sites. Remember that filters aren't always foolproof – sites and users can get around them – so do stay involved. www.getnetwise.org reviews different filtering tools.

- Talk with your children and agree what kinds of sites are safe. Check regularly to make sure that they stay within these agreed limits. You should always have a good idea of what your children are doing online and who they are talking to. Keep communication open and make sure your child knows it's never too late to tell someone if something is wrong or makes them feel uncomfortable.

- Tell your child to keep their identity private; they should not share personal information, including name, address, phone numbers, name of school or messenger id to anyone over the net. Use of an online nickname can help here, as long as they don't pretend to be a completely different person. If they send or publish pictures or videos of themselves or their families and friends they need to be aware that these can be changed and shared by anyone.

- If your child receives spam/junk email or texts, remind them never to believe them, reply to them or use them. It is best to delete files and attachments from unknown senders which can contain viruses or worse – inappropriate images or films. Visit www.childnet-int.org/sorted for advice on how to protect yourself online and install various protection software such as anti-virus, anti-spy and pop-up blocker.

- Your children should not accept gifts (electronic or otherwise) from strangers, or arrange meetings with new friends unless you go with them. Help your child to understand that some people lie online and that therefore it's better to keep online friends online. They should never meet up with someone they've met online without first telling you or an adult they trust.

- Social networking sites are the main way to meet people online and can be lots of fun. But since they can be open to misuse, make sure your children are as cautious of strangers online as they would be in the world outside.

- If they see or receive any obscene, abusive or threatening messages, they shouldn't respond. They should save the content, let you know and you should consider reporting it – see below. Some chat rooms are moderated, so messages get screened to some extent, but this is not an absolute guarantee.

- Your children should know what to do if they come across anything bad. Teach them and yourself how to block someone online and to report illegal material to the Internet Watch Foundation.

- Remember that children may be able to access the internet via mobile phones, TVs and game consoles. It is important that your children understand that the same safety rules apply and that they should not give out their mobile number and any personal details to strangers and think carefully before sending on pictures of themselves. Encourage your children to talk to you if they are worried or receiving unwanted messages.

Help to protect young people from abuse

The following information is taken from the NSPCC booklet *Protecting children from sexual abuse*.

Child sexual abuse is when someone uses a child for his or her own sexual pleasure and gratification. An abuser may be a man or woman, or another child or adolescent. Both boys and girls can be abused, and sometimes from an early age.

Sexual abuse of children includes:

- sexual touching of any part of the body, clothed or unclothed, including using an object
- all penetrative sex, including penetration of the mouth with an object or part of the body
- encouraging a child to engage in sexual activity, including sexual acts with someone else, or making a child strip or masturbate
- intentionally engaging in sexual activity in front of a child or not taking proper measures to prevent a child being exposed to sexual activity by others
- meeting a child following sexual grooming, or preparation, with the intention of abusing them
- taking, making, permitting to take, distributing, showing or advertising indecent images of children
- paying for the sexual services of a child or encouraging them into prostitution or pornography
- showing a child images of sexual activity including photographs, videos or webcams.

Talking with your child about inappropriate touch

Help your child understand about sex, about his or her body and about what is sexually healthy. Talking about this can play an important part in protecting your child against abuse and developing your relationship with your child.

For example, your child needs to understand about private parts of the body in order to understand what is appropriate touching and what is not. Be as positive as possible – children should feel proud of their bodies and not ashamed. They also need to know that their bodies belong to them alone. These conversations are a normal part of parenting.

Build an open and trusting relationship with your child from when they are very young. Always listen carefully to their fears and concerns. It may be helpful to use the word surprise rather than secret in relation to birthday presents or family events. Help your child understand that it's okay to keep quiet about something such as a surprise birthday party, but not about anything that makes them feel unhappy or uncomfortable.

Teach your child they have the right to refuse to do anything they feel is wrong or that frightens them. Stress that they should not hesitate to tell you or another trusted adult or adult they know if something happens that they don't like.

How should I react if my child tells me that he or she has been sexually abused?

If your child has been sexually abused it is natural to feel a range of emotions but it is important that you do not react in a way that will add to your child's distress. Your child needs to know that he or she is not to blame. Make it clear that you do not doubt what they say. Allow your child to talk about what has happened, but do not force them to do so. Tell your child that they have done the right thing in telling you. Don't blame them if the abuse occurred because they disobeyed your instructions, for example, going out without your permission.

You may feel very confused, particularly if the abuser is a relative. You may want help in coping with powerful and conflicting emotions about the abuse. These could include shock, anger, disbelief, self-blame, disgust and fear.

Do not seek to confront the abuser yourself, instead contact social services, the NSPCC Child Protection Helpline or the police. You can find the number for social services in the local telephone directory for your area or on www.direct.gov.uk .

Useful organisations

- **fpa**
- Childline
- www.childnet-int.org
- www.getnetwise.org
- www.homeoffice.gov.uk
- www.iwf.org.uk
- NSPCC
- Parentline Plus
- Sex Education Forum
- Social services
- Suzy Lamplugh Trust

What do schools teach about sex and relationships?

CHAPTER 12

What this chapter covers

- What schools teach in England, Wales, Scotland and Northern Ireland.
- How you can become involved.

Although your child's school may provide sex and relationships education (SRE) it is important that you don't just leave it up to the school. Children spend far more time with you than at school and only a fraction of school time will be spent on SRE. Below, you will find a summary of SRE in schools. The law around SRE may change so for up-to-date information see **fpa**'s factsheets *Sex and relationships education* and *Relationships and sexuality education in Northern Ireland*.

England

- It is compulsory for all schools to teach some SRE in science lessons, covering topics including puberty, anatomy and human reproduction.
- All school governing bodies have to produce a policy statement on SRE in consultation with children, parents and staff. Primary schools' statements must describe their SRE programme or explain why it is not provided. Be aware that some primary schools do not teach about relationships as it is not compulsory.
- Secondary schools have to provide an SRE programme including, as a minimum, sexually transmitted infections, HIV and late stage HIV infection.

Although not required by law, most schools include other aspects of SRE within a wider personal, social and health education curriculum (PSHE). In October 2008 the Government announced that comprehensive SRE will be made compulsory as part of a statutory PSHE curriculum. However, it will be some time before this is introduced into schools.

Wales

Personal and social education (PSE) is part of the compulsory basic curriculum in primary and secondary schools and includes topics such as relationships and health.

SRE is compulsory in secondary schools. All primary schools are required to have a policy describing their SRE programme or explaining why SRE is not provided.

Scotland

Although not required by law, all schools are expected to provide SRE. Guidance was produced in 2001 for local authorities and schools, which requires schools to provide SRE within a programme of PSHE and religious and moral education. However, this will vary between schools and you can contact your child's school for a copy of their programme.

Northern Ireland

In Northern Ireland SRE is referred to as relationships and sexuality education (RSE). RSE is a statutory component of personal development and home economics as well as the science curriculum in primary and post primary schools.

How you can become involved in the SRE policy of your child's school

The Government guidance throughout the UK states that SRE policies should be developed in consultation with parents, young people, teachers and governors.

You can support teachers and contribute to school SRE in several ways:

- Ask to see a copy of the SRE policy and/or a copy of the SRE programme for your child's year so you can support at home what the school is doing.

- Ask for or arrange a meeting with the school's PSHE Co-ordinator. You might find it easier to discuss SRE in small groups so class, year or Parent Teacher Association (PTA) sessions are ideal. Or you might prefer a less personal approach in a large meeting.

- Ask to see the resources used in the classroom. You might be able to borrow books or other resources to use with your child at home. If you disagree with some aspect of the SRE that your child is receiving or you think the school isn't tackling it well enough, make an appointment with the school's PSHE Co-ordinator to discuss this.

You can also talk with your child about what they are learning at school, and how they feel about the SRE they are receiving.

Useful organisations

- **fpa**
- Sex Education Forum

Useful organisations

This chapter includes information and contact details of organisations that offer further information and support on sex and relationships or other topics brought up in this book.

How fpa can help you

sexual health direct is a nationwide service run by **fpa**. It provides:

- confidential information and advice and a wide range of booklets on individual methods of contraception, common sexually transmitted infections, pregnancy choices, abortion and planning a pregnancy

- details of contraception, sexual health and genitourinary medicine (GUM) clinics and sexual assault referral centres.

fpa helplines

England
helpline 0845 122 8690
9am to 6pm Monday to Friday

Northern Ireland
helpline 0845 122 8687
9am to 5pm Monday to Thursday
9am to 4.30pm Friday

or visit **fpa**'s website www.fpa.org.uk

Unplanned pregnancy in Northern Ireland

If you are faced with an unplanned pregnancy and you live in Northern Ireland, **fpa** in Northern Ireland can offer:

- non-judgmental and non-directive counselling

- information on all your options to help you decide what to do.

fpa in Northern Ireland also offers a counselling service for women who have had an abortion.

Find out more. For an appointment, call **fpa** in Northern Ireland on 0845 122 8687. The service is confidential.

Your child's school

You can always contact your child's school and ask to see a copy of the SRE policy and/or a copy of the SRE programme for your child's year so you can support at home what the school is doing. See Chapter 12 for more information.

Action for Kids
Tel: 0845 300 0237
www.actionforkids.org
Works with disabled children and young people, their parents and carers to help to remove the barriers to independence.

Alcohol Concern
Tel: 020 7264 0510
www.alcoholconcern.org.uk
Offers a range of services to people with alcohol related problems.

Ann Craft Trust, The
Tel: 0115 9515400
www.anncrafttrust.org
Works to safeguard children and adults with learning disabilities who may be at risk of abuse and provides information for parents and carers.

www.avert.org
You'll find teen pages on this HIV and late stage HIV website.

www.bbc.co.uk/barefacts
Everything parents ever wanted their child to know about sex, love and relationships but were too embarrassed to ask.

beat
Tel: 0845 634 1414
www.b-eat.co.uk
For concerns about weight and eating.

bpas
Tel: 08457 30 40 30
www.bpas.org
Information and advice on pregnancy and pregnancy choices, including abortion.

British Association for Adoption and Fostering
Tel: 020 7421 2600
www.baaf.org.uk
Advice and information about adoption and fostering in the UK.

British Institute of Learning Disabilities
Tel: 01562 723010
www.bild.org.uk
Working to improve the lives of people with learning disabilities in the UK through research, training and working with advocacy groups.

Brook
Tel: 0800 0185 023
www.brook.org.uk
Clinics offering sexual health advice and contraception for young people up to the age of 25.

Calthorpe Clinic
Tel: 0121 455 7585
www.calthorpe-clinic.co.uk
Provides abortion services for both private and NHS clients.

Childline
Tel: 0800 11 11
www.childline.org.uk
A helpline for children and young people dealing with any issue.

www.childnet-int.org
A charity working to make the internet a safer place for children.

www.condomessentialwear.co.uk
Tel: 0800 567 123
Free sexual health helpline and website, with information about sexually transmitted infections and how to protect against them, and details of genitourinary medicine (GUM) and sexual health clinics.

Connexions
Tel: 080 800 13219
www.connexions.gov.uk
Information and advice for 13–19 year olds.

Contact a Family
Tel: 0808 808 355
www.cafamily.org.uk
Provides advice, information and support to parents of disabled children.

Department for Children, Schools and Families
Tel: 0870 000 2288
www.dcsf.gov.uk
Government department with information on schools and parenting.

Drinkaware
Tel: 020 7307 7450
www.drinkaware.co.uk
Information and advice about drinking alcohol safely and cutting down.

www.eatwell.gov.uk
Information on healthy eating for all ages and stages of life, including teenagers and pregnancy.

Education for Choice
Tel: 020 7249 3535
www.efc.org.uk
Information about abortion and practical advice for young people and parents.

Every Child Matters
Tel: 0870 000 2288
www.everychildmatters.gov.uk
Government information on young people's services including education, culture, social care and justice.

Family and Parenting Institute, The
Tel: 020 7424 3460
www.familyandparenting.org
Supports parents in bringing up their children and has a range of resources for parents.

FFLAG (Families and Friends of Lesbians and Gays)
Tel: 0845 652 0311
www.fflag.org.uk
Supports parents and their gay, lesbian and bisexual sons and daughters. Has a network of local parents' groups and contacts.

Foundation for people with learning disabilities
Tel: 020 7803 1111
www.learningdisabilities.org.uk
Works with people with learning disabilities, their families and people who care for them.

Frank
Tel: 0800 77 66 00
www.talktofrank.com
Confidential drugs information and where to go for help.

Get connected
Tel: 0808 808 4994
www.getconnected.org.uk
Confidential help and support for young people in difficult situations. They will put young people in touch with appropriate services.

www.getnetwise.org.uk
Resources to help people to use the internet safely.

Go Smoke Free
Tel: 0800 022 4332
www.gosmokefree.nhs.uk
Information about free NHS services to help people stop smoking.

www.homeoffice.gov.uk
Information on sexual assault referral centres.

www.itsnotyourfault.org
Information for children and young people about divorce and separation.

www.iwf.org.uk
Information on how to report websites you are concerned about.

www.likeitis.org.uk
Access to information about all aspects of sex and relationships education and teenage life.

London Lesbian and Gay Switchboard
Tel: 020 7837 7324
www.llgs.org.uk
Services for lesbians, gay men and bisexuals.

Marie Stopes
Tel: 0845 300 8090
www.mariestopes.org.uk
Information and advice on sexual health, including abortion.

Mencap
Tel: 020 7454 0454
www.mencap.org.uk
Information for people with a learning disability and their families.

National Childbirth Trust
Tel: 0870 444 8709
www.nct.org.uk
Information on pre-pregnancy care and health of pregnant women, local antenatal classes, postnatal support groups and breastfeeding counsellors.

NSPCC
Tel: 0808 800 5000
www.nspcc.org.uk
Counselling, information and advice to anyone concerned about a child at risk of abuse.

NHS Direct
Tel: 0845 46 47 (England and Wales)/
NHS 24 on 08454 242424 (Scotland)
www.nhsdirect.nhs.uk
Information on health and treatments.

Parentline Plus
Tel: 0808 800 2222
www.parentlineplus.org.uk
Help and advice on all aspects of
bringing up children.

www.parentscentre.gov.uk
Information and support on how to help
with your child's learning.

Relate
Tel: 0845 456 1310
www.relate.org.uk
Provides free counselling for young
people whose parents are separating.

**Royal College of Obstetricians and
Gynaecologists**
www.rcog.org.uk
Provides patient information on various
topics, including abortion and health
during pregnancy.

Sex Education Forum
Tel: 020 7843 1901
www.ncb.org.uk/sef
Information about sex and relationships
education in schools.

Sexual Health Line
Tel: 0800 567 123
24-hour advice on all aspects of
sexually transmitted infections.

Sexwise
Tel: 0800 28 29 30
www.ruthinking.co.uk
Sexual health information for young
people.

Social services
You can find the number for social
services in the local telephone
directory for your area or on
www.direct.gov.uk which lists all
public services, including social
services.

South Manchester Private Clinic
Tel: 0161 487 2660
www.smpclinic.co.uk
A private clinic providing pregnancy
advice and abortions.

Stonewall
Tel: 08000 50 20 20
www.stonewall.org.uk
Charity working for equality
and justice for gay, lesbian and
bisexual people.

Supportline
Tel: 020 8554 9004
www.supportline.org.uk
Emotional support for those who
are socially isolated, vulnerable,
at risk and victims of abuse,
including bullying, violence, sexual
assault and rape.

Suzy Lamplugh Trust
Tel: 020 7091 0074
www.suzylamplugh.org
Practical support to develop skills and
strategies for keeping safe.

Terrence Higgins Trust
Tel: 0845 1221 200
www.tht.org.uk
Information on safer sex, HIV and late
stage HIV infection.

www.there4me.com
Support for 12–16 year olds on issues
such as abuse, bullying and drugs.

Tommy's the Baby Charity
Tel: 0870 777 3060
www.tommys.org
Information and publications on
pre-pregnancy health, pregnancy,
miscarriage and stillbirth.

Trust for the Study of Adolescence
Tel: 01273 693311
www.studyofadolescence.org.uk
Research and information on teenagers
and young adults.

Working Families
Tel: 0800 013 0313
www.workingfamilies.org.uk
Information and help for parents
and families on all aspects of working
and family life.

www.youngminds.org.uk
Information for young people on
mental health and wellbeing.

Youth Access
Tel: 020 8772 9900
www.youthaccess.org.uk
Young people's information, advice,
counselling and support services.

CHAPTER 14

Useful resources

Resources for parents and carers from fpa

fpa sells a range of information suitable for parents and carers to use with their children or for young people to look at on their own.

Parents' pack

The neat case is designed to sit on a bookshelf and comes with a copy of our popular booklet for parents and carers *Talking to your child about sex and relationships* and **fpa**'s range of hugely successful booklets for young people – *4You: growing up*, *Periods*, *4Boys*, *4Girls*, *Abortion*, *Is everybody doing it?*, *Pregnancy*, *Love S.T.I.ngs* and *Love sex relationships*.

Talking to your child about sex and relationships

The booklet is packed with support for parents and carers of children of all ages who want to talk comfortably with their children about sex and relationships.

Let's grow with Nisha and Joe

In this comic, Nisha, Joe and their dog gently introduce 6–7 year olds to the concepts of growth and physical change, using reassuring stories and pictures.

4You: growing up … what's it all about?

Straightforward information on puberty and growing up for young people aged nine and above.

Periods: what you need to know

Colourful booklet for young people aged nine and above which prepares girls for their periods.

4Boys: a below-the-belt guide to the male body

A humorous, colourful, fully illustrated booklet for young people aged 12 and above.

4Girls: a below-the-bra guide to the female body

A colourful booklet for young people aged 12 and above which tells them all they want to know about physical changes and sexual development.

Is everybody doing it? Your guide to contraception

An illustrated booklet for young people aged 12 and above, dealing with peer pressure, starting a sexual relationship, contraception and sexually transmitted infections.

Love S.T.I.ngs: a beginner's guide to sexually transmitted infections

Comic strip style booklet for young people aged 12 and above which answers their questions about sexually transmitted infections.

Pregnancy: a young person's guide
A realistic view of pregnancy for young people aged 12 and above.

Abortion: just so you know
Accurate information about abortion for young people aged 12 and above.

Love sex relationships
A colourful booklet to help young people aged 12 and above explore how they feel about their own sexuality, body image and relationships.

Is this love?
A pocket sized booklet to help young people aged 14 and above identify, and protect against, abusive behaviour.

Love sex life
Supports young people aged 16 and above who want to explore all aspects of sex and relationships.

All about us
A CD-ROM for people with learning disabilities to use on their own or with support. Covers growing up and personal and sexual relationships.

Talking together
… about growing up
… about sex and relationships
… about contraception
Our series of three books about sexual health, for use with young people with learning disabilities.

Mummy laid an egg (mini-version)
Babette Cole (Random House)
A humorous twist on sex and relationships education as children tell their parents the facts about reproduction. Brilliantly illustrated and imaginative book. For children aged six and above.

Let's talk about where babies come from
Robie H Harris, illustrated by Michael Emberley (Walker books)
Answers many of the questions children have about babies, bodies, love, sex, reproduction and families. Full of colourful illustrations to keep children interested. For children aged 8–12.

Let's talk about sex
Robie H Harris, illustrated by Michael Emberley (Walker Books)
Thorough, frank and up-to-date information on all aspects of growing up, puberty, sex and sexual health. Covers both biology and emotions, and includes information on contraception and parts of the body. For children aged 10–14 years.

Factsheets
Sex and relationships education
Relationships and sexuality education in Northern Ireland
Explores all you need to know about SRE and RSE in schools.

To order:

Visit www.fpa.org.uk or contact **fpa** for a publications catalogue.
Tel: 0845 122 8600
Fax: 0845 123 2349
Email: fpadirect@fpa.org.uk

Resources from other organisations

There are also lots of useful resources produced by other organisations which you can use with your children:

- Blume J, **Letters to Judy**
  (Macmillan Children's Books, 1996).

- Cole B, **Hair in funny places**
  (Red Fox, 2001).

- Fisher N, **Living with a willy**
  (Macmillan Children's Books, 1994).

- Gravelle K, **The period book**
  (Piatkus, 1997).

- Madaras L, **What's happening to my body? Book for boys**
  (Newmarket Press, 2008).

- Madaras L, **What's happening to my body? Book for girls**
  (Newmarket Press, 2008).

- Mayle P, **Where did I come from?**
  (Macmillan Children's Books, 2006).

- McCall D and Naik A, **Let's talk sex**
  (Random House, 2007).

- Meredith S, **Growing up**
  (Usborne, 1997).

- Meredith S, **Where do babies come from?**
  (Usborne, 1991).

- Pavanel J, **The sex book: no nonsense guide for teenagers**
  (Wizard, 2003).

- Stoppard M, **Questions children ask**
  (Dorling Kindersley, 2001).

Speakeasy

The Trust for the Study of Adolescence conducted a five-year evaluation of **fpa**'s Speakeasy course. This evaluation found that the course improved parents' knowledge and confidence in talking with their children about sex and relationships.

Parents were asked to rate their own confidence in talking with their child before the Speakeasy course and after the course. On average, confidence levels were 47 per cent higher after the course.

Before taking the course, 61 per cent of parents said they agreed or strongly agreed with the statement, 'I feel able to talk to my children openly about sex'. After the course this had risen to 95.5 per cent.

Before the course, 60 per cent agreed or strongly agreed with the statement, 'I am aware of opportunities to raise issues with my children'. After the course this had risen to 97 per cent.

Parents reported that Speakeasy had a direct impact on their ability to respond confidently to their children in an age-appropriate way in situations where, before the course, they would not have felt able to do so. Comments from parents who have taken the course are below.

"My son has been asking what sperm is and how it's made – I told him as much as I could – like the purpose of sperm, where it's stored and stuff, but I didn't know how it was made. Before the course I would have been embarrassed and probably tried to ignore the question, now I am able to tell him that although I don't know the answer, I now know where I can get the information. I still don't know the answer, but he knows that as soon as I find out I will tell him."

"I will now tackle questions head-on rather than ignoring them or changing the subject. I try to answer as well as I can and in as much detail as I can."

"I just told him about anal sex, and I didn't even get embarrassed! I remembered from the course to say that some people do it and that's okay, but he doesn't have to!"

Speakeasy

- Do you feel comfortable and relaxed talking with your children about growing up?

- Want to be more prepared for the kind of questions your children may ask?

- Could you use some support?

Speakeasy is a fun and relaxed course for mums, dads and carers of children of all ages. It will help you build on what you already know about sex and relationships and offers you the opportunity to learn together using your own experiences. Courses are delivered by skilled **fpa** trainers in small and friendly groups.

How do I find out more about Speakeasy?

If you are a mum, dad or carer and want to go on a Speakeasy course in your area, contact **fpa**:

Tel: **020 7608 5243**
Email: speakeasy@fpa.org.uk
www.fpa.org.uk

Index